# Inside the TV Jungle—

where an instinct for the jugular is necessary for survival, especially if the network ratings are going down . . .

And they were plummeting on the UBS-TV nightly newscast. The aging, boozing anchorman, Howard Beale, would have to go. As a farewell to his dwindling audience, Howard made his parting gesture: calmly, politely, with just the right amount of charisma, he announced that he would kill himself exactly a week from that night—during his broadcast!

This "grotesque little incident," as the executive senior vice-president called it, sent the ratings soaring. And with a wisdom born of infinite greed, the gorgeous program director turned Howard into the top-rated news sensation of TV.

Then Howard began to hear voices; he became the mad prophet of the airways. Now, the network biggies decided, Howard *would* have to go—permanently. And there was only one efficient way to eliminate him!

# NETWORK

Novelization by
## SAM HEDRIN

Screenplay by
## PADDY CHAYEFSKY

A KANGAROO BOOK
PUBLISHED BY POCKET BOOKS NEW YORK

NETWORK

POCKET BOOK edition published December, 1976
5th printing ........................ April, 1977

This original POCKET BOOK edition is printed from brand-new
plates made from newly set, clear, easy-to-read type.
POCKET BOOK editions are published by
POCKET BOOKS,
a Simon & Schuster Division of
GULF & WESTERN CORPORATION
1230 Avenue of the Americas,
New York, N.Y. 10020.
Trademarks registered in the United States
and other countries.

# NETWORK

# CHAPTER 1

This story is about Howard Beale, the network news anchorman on UBS-TV. In his time, Howard Beale had been a mandarin of television, the grand old man of news, with a HUT rating of 16 and a 28 audience share. He was fifty-eight years old, silver-haired, magisterial, dignified to the point of divinity. In 1969, however, he fell to a 22 share and, by 1972, he was down to a 15 share. In 1973, his wife died and he was left a childless widower with an 8 rating and a 12 share. He became morose and isolated, began to drink heavily, and, on September 23, 1974, he was fired, effective in two weeks. The news was broken to him by Max Schumacher, who was the president of the News Division at United Broadcasting Systems and an old friend. The two men went out and got appropriately drunk. By two o'clock in the morning, they were so sodden they were almost sober.

"I'm going to kill myself," Howard said.

"Oh, shit, Howard," said Max.

"I'm going to blow my brains out right on the air, right in the middle of the seven o'clock news, like that girl in Florida a couple of months ago."

"You'll get a hell of a rating," Max said, "I'll tell you that, a fifty share, easy."

"You think so?"

"We could make a series out of it. 'Suicide of the Week.' Hell, why limit ourselves? 'Execution of the Week'—'The Madame Defarge Show'! Every Sunday night, bring your knitting and watch somebody get guillotined, hung, electrocuted, gassed. For a logo, we'll have some brute with a black hood over his head. Think of the spinoffs—'*Rape* of the Week' . . ."

Howard began to get caught up in the idea. " 'Terrorist of the Week'?"

"Beautiful!"

"How about 'Coliseum '74'?" Howard said. "Every week we throw some Christians to the lions!"

"Fantastic! 'The Death Hour'! I love it! Suicides, assassinations, mad bombers, Mafia hitmen, murder in the barbershop, human sacrifices in witches' covens, automobile smashups. 'The Death Hour'! A great Sunday night show for the whole family. We'll wipe Disney right off the air."

They sniggered and snorted. Howard Beale laid his head down on the booth's table, fighting sleep.

The next morning, Howard's housekeeper found her employer still wearing the clothes he had worn the night before, curled in a position of fetal helplessness on the floor in the far corner of the room.

"Are you all right, Mr. Beale?" she called.

Howard opened one eye. "I'm fine, thank you, Mrs. Merryman." With some effort he managed to get to his feet.

The rest of the day was seemingly routine. Howard was in his office by nine as always, a small, unpretentious fifth-floor office, cluttered with books, magazines, periodicals and photographs and awards on the walls, mementos. He quickly typed his copy for that evening's broadcast, then paused to pour himself a quick shot of Scotch. He made his regular trips out to the main news room to check his facts in reference books and took a few telephone calls from the UBS bureaus in Washington and San Francisco. He generally had a glass of Scotch with him, but that wasn't unusual. He seemed sober enough at the daily rundown meeting, which took place at one o'clock.

It was Tuesday, September 24, 1974, and you may recall the news that day had to deal with a Kissinger speech before the United Nations and Nelson Rockefeller's hearings before the Senate Rules Committee on his nomination for the vice-presidency. Everyone at the rundown meeting remembers Howard as being alert, even brisk. Certainly no one suspected anything was wrong. Not the makeup man who gave him a few last whisks of the brush and combed his hair, not the assistant producer, nor the floor manager of the news show, who watched from the floor of the studio as Howard put on his jacket for the show, prepared his copy and waited for a cue from the director in the control room to begin the show. In fact, the first ten minutes of the program were routine.

Up in the control room the clock read 6:39. (It was actually "The Seven O'Clock News"; the show went out live to sixty-seven affiliated stations at 6:30, and the tape was played by the affiliates that carried the show at 7:00.) It was a typical control room with a room-length double bank of television monitors, including two color monitor screens, the show monitor and the pre-set monitor. Before this array of TV screens the director sat, flanked on his left by the production assistant who stop-watched the show, and on his right by a technical director. To the right of the technical director sat the lighting director. For the moment, these people were watching the show monitor, on which appeared Jack Snowden, the network's Washington correspondent, who was doing a lead-in to his report on the second day of the Rockefeller hearings.

SNOWDEN: Rockefeller again supported President Ford's pardon of former President Nixon . . .

The technical director murmured into his mike, "Twenty-four . . ."

SNOWDEN: . . . as an act of conscience . . .

Now the director murmured into his mike, "Lou, kick that little thing shut on ground level . . ."

# NETWORK

SNOWDEN: . . . an act of compassion . . .

The show monitor screen switched to film of Nelson Rockefeller testifying before the Rules Committee. Snowden's voice continued over this scene.

SNOWDEN: . . . and an act of courage . . .

"Forty seconds," the production assistant whispered.

"Twenty seconds to one," the director said softly into his mike.

On the monitor, Rockefeller was speaking, "The constitutional process worked . . ."

"Headroll," the director said, "rolling."

"The information was brought out," Rockefeller continued.

"Twenty-five," said the technical director, "twenty-six."

"The president resigned," Rockefeller said.

In the back of the control room, Harry Hunter, the executive producer, was flirting with his secretary.

"How the hell do you always get mixed up with married men?" he asked her.

The director overheard and leaned back to address himself to the secretary. "Sheila, if you're hot for married men, why go to strangers? What's wrong with me?"

Rockefeller's voice came over the monitor, "The president accepted a pardon . . ."

"Ten seconds," the production assistant said.

The director leaned back to his mike. "Ten seconds coming to one."

". . . which in my opinion . . ." Rockefeller said.

"And . . ." said the director.

". . . was tantamount to admitting guilt," said Rockefeller.

"One!" the director said.

Howard Beale's image suddenly flipped on-screen.

"Fifteen seconds to commercial freeze," said the production assistant.

"Headroll," the director said.

"Rolling," the technical director answered. And then they both turned in their seats to gossip briefly with Harry Hunter and his secretary.

Meanwhile, Howard Beale's voice issued from the monitor.

BEALE: Ladies and gentlemen, I would like at this moment to announce that I will be retiring from this program in two weeks time because of poor ratings . . .

The director whispered something to Harry Hunter's secretary which occasioned sniggers from her and from Harry Hunter.

BEALE: And since this show was the only thing I had going for me in my life, I have decided to kill myself . . .

Harry Hunter's secretary murmured something that caused him to burst into laughter.

BEALE: I'll tell you what I'm going to do.

I'm going to blow my brains out right on this program a week from today. . . .

Frowning and puzzled over this diversion from the script, the production assistant spoke into her mike, "Ten seconds to commercial freeze. . . ."

BEALE: So tune in next Tuesday. That'll give the public-relations people a week to promote the show, and we ought to get a hell of a rating with that, a fifty share, easy. . . .

Bewildered, the production assistant nudged the director.

"Listen, did you hear that?" she asked.

"And *two*," the director said into his mike.

The monitor screen erupted into a commercial for a cat food chow-chow-chow.

The audio man, leaning into the room from his glassed-in cubicle, called out, "What was that about?"

"Howard just said he was going to blow his brains out next Tuesday," the production assistant said to the director.

"What're you talking about?"

"Didn't you hear him?" she insisted. "He just said—"

Harry Hunter leaned forward to intervene. "What's wrong now?"

"Howard just said he was going to kill himself next Tuesday," the production assistant repeated.

"What do you mean Howard just said he was going to kill himself next Tuesday?"

The production assistant nervously riffled through her script. "He was supposed to do a tag on the Rockefeller-bump-commercial," she said.

"He said 'tune in next Tuesday,'" the audio man said, "'I'm going to shoot myself.'"

Everybody's attention now focused on the double bank of black-and-white monitor screens showing various parts of the studio, which was in an uproar.

The director got on his mike to his assistant director. "What the hell's going on?" he asked.

The assistant director, whose face could be seen on the monitor screen and whose voice boomed into the control room, said, "I don't know. He just said he was going to blow his brains out."

"What the hell's this all about, Howard?" the director asked into his mike.

Howard, visible on monitor, was shouting at floor personnel gathering around him. "Will you get the hell out of here? We'll be back on air in a couple of seconds!"

The director roared into his mike. "What the fuck's going on, Howard?"

"I can't hear you," Howard said, on monitor.

The director bawled to the audio man. "Put the studio mike on!"

"We're back on in eleven seconds," the audio man said.

"Ten seconds," said the production assistant.

Now Harry Hunter's voice boomed out into the studio. "Howard! What the hell are you doing? Have you flipped or what?"

The technical director murmured into his mike, "We start with thirty-one, thirty-two—"

Harry Hunter roared at the audio man. "Turn the mike off!"

The audio man came into the control room. "What the hell's going on?"

Harry Hunter raged. "Turn the fucking sound off, you stupid son of a bitch! This is going out live!"

The production assistant, her eye on her stopwatch, intoned, "Three, two, one—"

At that point the technical director pressed a button and the jangling cat food commercial flipped off the show monitor to be replaced at once by a scene of gathering bedlam around Howard's desk. The audio man fled in panic back to his cubicle to turn off the audio but not before Harry Hunter and the director, going out live to sixty-seven affliates, could be heard booming:

"Chrissakes! Black it out! This is going out live to sixty-seven fucking affiliates! Shit!"

"This," the director said, "is the fuckingest thing I ever saw!"

Up in his fifth-floor office, room 509, Max Schumacher stared petrified at the pandemonium he saw on his office console. He watched the assistant director and the associate producer and an electrician, as well, trying to pull Howard Beale away from his desk. Howard was trying to hit anyone he could with an ineffective right-hand haymaker.

BEALE: Get the fuck away from me!
OTHER VOICES FROM ALL DIRECTIONS: Cut the show! Get him out of there! Go to standby! For Chrissakes, you stupid—

Max's phone rang. He grabbed it and then replied, "How the hell do I know?" He hung up, grabbed another phone and barked, "Give me the network news control room!"

On the monitor screen hysteria clearly dominated. The screen suddenly leaped into a fragment of the cat food commercial, then a jarring shot of the bedlam on the studio floor. This particular camera seemed unattended as it panned dementedly back and forth, capturing the confusion on the studio floor. Then, abruptly, the screen filled with Vice-President-Designate Rockefeller testifying before the Senate Rules Committee.

Max shouted into the phone, "Black it out!"

The screen abruptly went black as Max slammed down his phone. His phone rang again but he was already headed for the door. The screen went to STANDBY and his squawk box blared.

"What the hell happened, Max?" a voice asked.

"How the hell do I know?" Max shouted as he made his exit. "I'm going down now!"

He strode into a large room where all the secretaries of the News Division executives have their desks. It was empty except for one secretary just putting the cover on her typewriter. Passing through that room he strode into the fifth-floor corridor, a long institutional passageway, part of an endless maze of similar corridors, with offices and technical rooms debouching on both sides. The corridor was beginning to fill up with News Division personnel who were working late, all of whom were either wondering what had happened or telling others what had happened. Max yanked an exit door open and disappeared down a flight of steps to emerge into the fourth-floor corridor and then into the studio.

Things seemed to have quieted down a bit; hysteria had given way to mumbles and murmurs and occasional laughter. Telephones rang shrilly and incessantly. In a far corner of the studio sat Howard Beale, surrounded by Harry Hunter, the director, the associate producer, the production assistant and the assistant director. Cameramen, grips and other floor personnel were gathered in clumps around the studio, murmuring and muttering and giggling over the whole absurd episode. Max headed straight for the group around Howard. They parted to let him in.

Harry Hunter saw Max and said, "Tom wants you to call as soon as you come in."

Max stared at Howard. A voice called out to Harry Hunter, "Harry! Joe Sweeney on the phone!"

Harry Hunter bawled back. "I'm not taking any more calls. Tell them Mr. Schumacher's here! They can talk to him!"

"Howard," Max said, staring at him, "you have got to be out of your everloving mind. Are you drunk?" He turned to the others. "How much boozing has he been doing today?"

Meanwhile, phones continued to ring and voices called out, "Harry! Thackeray wants to talk to you right now! Mr. Schumacher! Mr. Gianini wants to talk to you!"

Max said to Harry Hunter, "You better get hold of Mr. Chaney and Frank Hackett."

Three hours later, Frank Hackett came out of the elevator onto the fifth-floor corridor. Executive senior vice-president of the network, forty-one years old, Hackett was one of the new cool young breed of management. He had been called away from a dinner party in Westchester and was still wearing a tuxedo.

As he moved briskly through the corridor which was clotted with network executives, Hackett paused to address one executive. "Lou, can't we clear out that downstairs lobby? There must be a hundred people down there, every TV station and wire service in the city. I could barely get in."

"How am I going to clear them out, Frank?" the executive asked.

Hackett muttered and pushed his way into room 509, the executive office of the News Division. There he found Max Schumacher, the vice-president of the News Division, Robert McDonough; the vice-president in charge of public relations, Milton Steinman; the vice-president for legal affairs, Walter Gianini; the vice-president for owned-stations' news, Emil Dubrovnik; the general manager for news, radio, Michael Sandies; the vice-president for sales, Joe Donnelly; and others.

Joe Donnelly was on the phone. "How many spots were wiped out?" he asked.

Hackett addressed Gianini, who was studying a typescript of the aborted news show. "Anything litigable?"

"Not so far," Gianini said.

Donnelly continued on the phone. "We had to abort the show, Ed, what else could we do? We'll make good, don't worry about it."

Hackett turned to Arthur Zangwill, vice-president in charge of standards and practices. "Is Nelson in here?" he asked.

"He's talking to Wheeler," Zangwill said. "So far, over nine hundred phone calls complaining about the fucking foul language."

"Shit," Hackett muttered.

In the background, on another phone, a p.r. man was speaking. "Come on, Mickey, what page are you putting it on?"

Hackett crossed to Max's office which was jammed with, among others, Nelson Chaney, fifty-two, president of the network and every inch a patrician. He sat behind Max's desk talking on the phone and he looked up, noting Hackett's arrival.

"Frank Hackett just walked in," Chaney said.

Nearby, Milton Steinman, the vice-president in charge of public relations for the News Division, a rumpled, ordinarily amiable man in his early fifties, was talking on the phone to someone at CBS. "I can't release the tape, Marty," he said, "we're still studying it ourselves."

Another p.r. man stuck his head in the door and called to Steinman, "ABC again, wants the tape."

"Tell him to go fuck himself," Steinman said. Turning back to the phone, he added, "That goes for you too, Marty."

Hackett turned to Howard Beale who was sitting on the couch. "You're off the air as of now."

Chaney extended the phone to Hackett. "He wants to talk to you."

Before picking up the phone Hackett turned to Max Schumacher who was leaning against a wall. "Who's replacing Beale tomorrow?" he asked.

"We're flying up Snowden from Washington," Max said.

A young lawyer from Legal Affairs came in to give Walter Amundsen, general counsel of the network, a piece of paper.

He was immediately followed by Herb Thackeray, the vice-president for station relations. "I'm catching all kinds of hell," Thackeray said.

Hackett had picked up the phone. "John," he said, "we've got a stockholder's meeting tomorrow. This stupid thing is going to overshadow everything."

Steinman spoke to Max. "It is almost eleven o'clock, Max. Let's see how the other networks are handling this." He gestured at a bank of four television monitors, three on the wall and a large office console monitor of UBS-TV. Max leaned around Hackett who was now sitting in Max's chair and clicked on the monitors.

Hackett continued. "Walter's drafted a statement, I haven't seen it yet. I just got here, John, I was at a dinner party."

The four monitor screens erupted into a variety of commercials. Max toned the volume down.

"Hang on," Hackett said into the phone, "I want to see this."

"Channels 5 and 11 made it the opener," Steinman said.

Suddenly the faces of Dave Marash, Roger Smith, Chuck Scarborough, Roger Grimsby and Bill Beutel and the UBS local news anchorman, Tim Halloway, were on the screens announcing the stories that would be covered on that evening's late local news shows. All of them, in their own ways, made it clear that their lead story would be about Howard Beale's startling announcement of his own upcoming suicide. Norman Moldanian, vice-president of owned stations, entered the room. "This mess is going to cost us half a million bucks," he said.

Hackett, still holding the phone and concentrating on the monitors, said, Shut up, Norman."

In Milton Steinman's office a clump of network executives were all watching the four monitor screens on the wall. The opening commercials were coming to an end on all four sets. "I know 5 opened with it," somebody said.

In the common room of the news division executives were clogging the doorways of all the offices to watch the 11:00 news.

In Max's office, affable Dave Marash on the CBS monitor was saying, "An unusual thing happened at one of our sister networks, UBS, this evening. . . ."

Roger Grimsby on another monitor said, almost simultaneously, "Howard Beale, one of television's most esteemed newscasters . . ."

Chuck Scarborough, on a different monitor, said, "Howard Beale interrupted his network news program tonight to announce . . ."

"Shit," Hackett muttered.

Tim Halloway on another monitor was saying, "Secretary of State Henry Kissinger made a forceful address before the United Nations General Assembly. . . ."

Hackett spoke to Max, "How are we handling it?"

"Halloway's going to make a brief statement

21

at the end of the show," Max said, "to the effect Howard's been under great personal stress, et cetera."

Hackett reached to click off the bank of monitor screens, then he returned to his phone call. "I'll call you back, John," he said. He hung up the phone and turned to face the other executives. "All right. We've got a stockholders' meeting tomorrow at which the principal business will be the restructuring-of-management plan, and I don't want this grotesque incident to interfere with that. I'll suggest Mr. Ruddy open with a short statement washing this whole thing off, and you, Max, better have some answers in case some of those nuts that always come to stockholders' meetings . . ."

Max, leaning against the wall, said, "Mr. Beale has been under great personal and professional pressures. . . ."

Hackett exploded. "I've got some goddamn surprises for you too, Schumacher! I've had it up to here with your cruddy division and its annual thirty-three million dollar deficit!"

"Don't fuck around with my news division, Frank," Max said. "We're responsible to corporate level, not to you."

"We'll goddamn well see about that!" Hackett said.

"All right, take it easy," Chaney said. "Right now, how're we going to get Beale out of here? I understand there's at least a hundred reporters and camera crews in the lobby."

"We've got a limo waiting at the freight entrance," Max said. He turned to Howard Beale.

"I called Louise, Howard, and you'll stay at my place tonight. There's bound to be press around your place."

"Sure," Howard said.

# CHAPTER 2

On Wednesday morning at ten oclock, in his shirtsleeves and with the bright sunlight streaming in, Max Schumacher sat at his desk talking on the phone. "I want Snowden here by noon," he said. "Have Lester cover the Rockefeller hearings and give the White House to Doris."

His secretary stuck her head in. "You're late for your screening," she said.

Max hung up, gathered his jacket from a chair and headed for the door. "If John Wheeler calls," he said, "switch him to Screening Room Seven." Then he left.

There were two people already in Screening Room Seven on the ninth floor. They were Bill Herron, thirty-six, a whippet-like, casually dressed man, and Diana Christensen, dressed in slacks and blouse, thirty-four, tall, willowy, with the best ass ever seen on a vice-president in charge of programming.

"I'm sorry—this Beale business," Max said, on entering.

Max and Diana exchanged nods and professionally polite greetings. Herron buzzed the projectionist. "Diana asked if she could sit in on this," he explained.

"Fine," Max said, and called to Diana, "How's it going?"

She shrugged and smiled. The lights in the room dimmed and a shaft of light shot out from the projection room. The phone at Max's elbow buzzed. He answered it, talking softly into the phone.

"Max Schumacher—I'm glad I got you, John. Listen, I got into a hassle with Frank Hackett last night over the Howard Beale thing, and he made a crack about the stockholders' meeting this afternoon. He said something about having some surprises for me. Is there something going on I don't know about? . . . John, I'm counting on you and Mr. Ruddy to back me up against that son of a bitch. . . . Okay." He hung up and watched a documentary film that had just begun on the screen. He saw a handsome black woman in her early thirties.

"Who's that," Max asked, "Laureen Hobbs?"

"Yeah," Herron said.

Laureen Hobbs was sitting in a typical panel discussion grouping, flanked by three men and a woman, two white, two black, all very urban guerilla—in fatigues, sunglasses and combat boots. Miss Hobbs looked calmly into the camera and said, "The Communist Party believes that the most pressing political necessity today is the consolidation of the revolutionary, radical and democratic movements into a united front . . ."

The phone buzzed and Max picked it up. "Yeah? . . . Oh, goddamnit, when, Louise? . . . Well, did he say anything? . . . All right, thanks." He hung up and then promptly picked up the phone again. "4807," he said.

Laureen Hobbs continued on screen. "Repression is the response of an increasingly desperate, imperialist ruling clique. Indeed, the entire apparatus of the bourgeois-democratic state, especially its judicial system and its prisons, is disintegrating . . ."

"Harry," Max spoke into the phone, "Howard left my house about ten minutes ago presumably headed here. Let me know as soon as he gets here."

Laureen Hobbs was still on screen. "The fascist thrust must be resisted in its incipient stages by the broadest possible coalition . . ."

It went on like that for another twenty minutes. "What we're going to see now," Herron said, "is something really sensational. The Falstaff Independent Bank in Arizona was ripped off last week by a terrorist group called the Ecumenical Liberation Army, and they themselves actually took movies of the ripoff while they were ripping it off. It's in black-and-white, but wait'll you see it."

The screen suddenly erupted into film of the interior of a bank being entered by three men, two of them black, and two women, one black and one white. They dispersed to various parts of the bank as if they were there on legitimate business.

"The Ecumenical Liberation Army," Diana said. "Is that the one that kidnapped Patty Hearst?"

"No," Herron said, "that's the Symbionese Liberation Army. This is the Ecumenical Liberation Army. They're the ones who kidnapped Mary Ann Gifford three weeks ago. There's a hell of a lot of liberation armies in the revolutionary underground and a lot of kidnapped heiresses. That's Mary Ann Gifford." This last reference was to a young white woman on screen who was lugging a shopping bag as she joined a line at the teller's window.

"You mean they actually shot this film while they were ripping off the bank?" Diana said.

"Yeah, wait'll you see it," Herron said. "I don't know whether to edit or leave it raw like this. That's the Great Ahmed Khan; he's the leader."

On screen, the film went out of, then back into focus, bounced meaninglessly around the bank, then finally settled on a large, powerful black man at one of the desks, presumably writing out a series of deposit slips.

"This is terrific stuff," Diana said. "Where did you get it?"

"I got everything through Laureen Hobbs," Herron said. "She's my contact for all this stuff."

"I thought she was straight Communist Party."

"Right, but she's trying to unify all the factions in the underground, so she knows everybody."

On screen the camera panned aimlessly, focusing and unfocusing, picking up Mary Ann Gifford bending over her shopping bag and pulling out a Czech service submachine gun 9 Parabellum which she pointed at the ceiling. The film was silent, but the reactions of everyone around suggested clearly that she had fired the gun. The film got fragmented and panicky, along with the activity in the bank. Max's phone buzzed and he picked it up. "Yeah?" Max said. "All right, put him on."

In the nightly news room Harry Hunter was sitting at an empty desk with the phone in his hand. He leaned back and called to Howard Beale, "Howard—I've got Max on four, would you pick up?"

Howard Beale, sitting in his own office, picked up the phone. "Listen, Max," he said, "I'd like another shot—"

"Oh, come on, Howard," Max said, watching the frenetic bank robbery footage going on.

"I don't mean the whole show. I'd just like to come on, make some kind of brief farewell statement and then turn the show over to Jack Snowden. I have eleven years at this network, Max. I have some standing in this industry. I don't want to go out like a clown. It'll be simple and dignified. You and Harry can check the copy."

Harry Hunter, listening in on the call from another phone, broke in. "I think it'll take the strain off the show, Max. How much time do you want, Howard?"

"A minute forty-five, maybe two."

"All right, I'll give you two on the top and then we'll go to Jack Snowden with the Kissinger UN speech."

In Screening Room Seven the show was over and the lights went on. Max said into the phone, "And no booze today, Howard."

He noticed Diana and Herron moving to the

door, waving goodbyes. Max waved slackly in return. He couldn't help watching Diana as she walked out.

"No booze," Howard said into the phone. He hung up and sat for a moment, scowling and making curious grimaces. Then he stood, removed his jacket and dumped it on a chair. He rolled his sleeves up and suddenly made a strange grunt. He sat behind his desk, fitted a piece of paper into the machine and then, again, suddenly, growled.

As she made her way through the news room, the production assistant heard the strange noises coming from Howard Beale's office. She paused in his doorway. "You all right, Mr. Beale? You want me to close your door?"

He nodded, typing, grunting, growling.

She closed his door.

On the fourteenth floor Diana and Herron came out of the elevator and turned left through the glass doors marked DEPARTMENT OF PROGRAMMING. As she moved through the suite of offices, Diana paused to look into one of them. "George, can you come in my office for a minute?"

She continued until she reached her own office, hailing her assistant on the way. "Barbara, is Tommy around?"

"I think so," Barbara said.

"I'd like to see the two of you for a moment." Diana entered her office followed by Herron. She skimmed through her messages. The office was executive-size, windows looking out on canyons of glass and stone. Her desk was piled high with scripts. George Basch, vice-president for program development, East Coast, a slight, balding man of thirty-nine, entered, nodded to Herron and took a seat. He was followed by Barbara Schlesinger, head of the story department, and Tommy Pellegrino, assistant vice-president, programs, thirty-six, swarthy, expensively coiffed, and mustachioed. All, except Herron, seated themselves.

Diana made the short introductions, then said, "Look, I just saw some rough footage of a special Bill's doing on the revolutionary underground. Most of it's tedious stuff of Laureen Hobbs and four fatigue jackets muttering mutilated Marxism. But he's got about eight minutes of a bank robbery that is absolutely sensational. Authentic stuff. Actually shot while the robbery was going on. Remember the Mary Ann Gifford kidnapping? Well, it's that bunch of nuts. She's in the film shooting off machine guns. Really terrific footage. I think we can get a hell of a movie of the week out of it, maybe even a series."

"A series of what?" Pellegrino wanted to know. "What're we talking about?"

"Look," Diana said. "We've got a bunch of hobgoblin radicals called the Ecumenical Liberation Army who go around taking home movies of themselves kidnapping heiresses, hijacking 747s, bombing bridges, assassinating ambassadors. We'd open each week's segment with that authentic footage, hire a couple of writers to write some story behind that footage, and we've got ourselves a series."

"A series about a bunch of bank-robbing guerillas?" Basch said.

"What are we going to call it," Schlesinger asked, " 'The Mao Tse-tung Hour'?"

"Why not?" Diana said. "They've got 'Strike Force,' 'Task Force,' 'SWAT,' why not Che Guevara and his own little mod squad? Listen, I sent you all a concept analysis research report yesterday. Did any of you read it?"

There was no sign that anyone had.

"Well, in a nutshell," she continued, "it said the American people are turning sullen. They've been clobbered on all sides by Vietnam, Watergate, inflation, the depression. They've turned off, shot up, and they've fucked themselves limp. And nothing helps. Evil still triumphs over all, Christ is a dope-dealing pimp, even sin turned out to be impotent. The whole world seems to be going nuts and flipping off into space like an abandoned balloon. So—this concept analysis report concludes—the American people want somebody to articulate their rage for them. I've been telling you people since I took this job six months ago that I want angry shows. I don't want conventional programming on this network. I want counterculture. I want anti-establishment." She paused and closed the door.

"Now," she resumed. "I don't want to play butch boss with you people. But when I took over this department it had the worst programming record in television history. This network hasn't one show in the top twenty. This network is an industry joke. We better start putting together one winner for next September. I want a show developed, based on the activities of a terrorist group. Joseph Stalin and his merry band of Bolsheviks. I want ideas from you people. And by the way, the next time I send an audience research report around, you all better read it, or I'll sack the fucking lot of you, is that clear?"

She paused, waiting for reactions. Then she turned to Herron. "I'll be out on the Coast in four weeks. Can you set up a meeting with Laureen Hobbs for me?"

"Sure," Herron said.

At three o'clock in a banquet room of the New York Hilton, the UBS stockholders' meeting was in progress. There was standing room only, with some two hundred stockholders seated and many others standing around the walls. On the rostrum, a phalanx of network executives were seated in three rows. These included Edward Ruddy, chairman of the board; John Wheeler, president of the broadcast group; the presidents and senior vice-presidents of the other divisions and other groups—the UBS records group, the UBS publishing group, the UBS theater chain, etc. Representing the network were Nelson Chaney, George Nichols, Norman Moldanian, Walter Amundsen, Max Schumacher and Frank Hackett—who was at the lectern, making the annual report. He droned.

". . . plan submitted to the Board was a reorganization with a view to the passing on of command and with the intention of creating a subcorporate second line of authority . . ."

Max Schumacher, bored with the proceedings, whispered to Nelson Chaney, who was seated beside him. The sixty-seven-year-old Edward Ruddy, the silver-haired Brahmin of Television, sat in the front row.

". . . for the supervision and coordination of the main profit centers," Hackett went on, "the acquisition of the United Broadcasting Systems by the Communications Corporation of America was approved by the FCC with the stipulation that UBS-TV remain a substantially autonomous subsidiary of CCA. . . . But the business of management is management; and UBS-TV is at this moment foundering with less than seven percent of national television revenues, most network programs being sold at station rates. The most obvious instance of mismanagement is the News Division . . ."

Max began to pay attention.

". . . with its 98 million dollar budget and its average annual deficit of 32 million. It is inconceivable that such a wanton fiscal affront go unresisted. . . . Accordingly, we submit a plan in which local news would be transferred to Owned Stations Divisions . . ."

Max stared angrily down his row toward Norman Moldanian, who studiously avoided his eye.

"News radio would be transferred to the UBS Radio Division . . ."

Max turned in his seat to scowl at George Nichols in the row behind him.

". . . and in effect, the News Division would be reduced in status . . ."

Max tried to catch the eye of Edward Ruddy but he stared stonily ahead.

". . . from that of a division to that of a department accountable to the network . . ."

Max was about ready to blow his stack.

At 5:30 P.M. the stockholders' meeting was over. The floor was a swirling crush of stockholders mingling with executives. Max Schumacher elbowed his way through the crowded aisle to get to where Edward Ruddy was chatting with a couple of stockholders.

Max touched Ruddy's arm. "What was that all about?" he asked.

"This is not the time, Max," Ruddy said urbanely.

Max was barely able to contain himself. "Why wasn't I told about this? Why was I led onto that podium and publicly guillotined in front of the stockholders? Goddamnit, I spoke to John Wheeler this morning, and he assured me the News Division was safe. Are you trying to get me to resign? It's a hell of a way to do it."

"We'll talk about this tomorrow at our regular morning meeting," Ruddy said smoothly. Max wheeled away in a rage.

He made it back to his office in a gathering rage. He took off his jacket, threw it on the couch and sat there. But he was too angry to stay there. He grabbed his jacket and took off for the news studio. The usual crew was present when Max entered and they looked up, giving him questioning glances. It was not customary for the president of the News Division to be present.

"Five seconds," the production assistant said.

"Picture's too thick," the lighting director said.

"Coming two—and one," said the director.

The show monitor which had been showing color patterns suddenly flicked on to show Howard Beale looking up from a sheaf of papers on his desk:

BEALE: Good evening. Today is Wednesday, September the twenty-fifth, and this is my last broadcast. Yesterday I announced on this program that I would commit public suicide, admittedly an act of madness. Well, I'll tell you what happened—I just ran out of bullshit . . .

"All right, cut him off," Harry Hunter said. The monitor screen went black.
"Leave him on," Max said from the back wall.
Howard Beale's image promptly flicked back on again.

BEALE: Am I still on the air?

Everybody in the control room looked to Max. "If this is how he wants to go out," Max said, "this is how he goes out."

BEALE: I don't know any other way to say it except I just ran out of bullshit . . .

A phone rang. Hunter answered it. Another phone rang. His secretary answered that.
"Look Mr. Schumacher's right here," Hunter said. "Do you want to talk to him?" He handed the phone to Max.

BEALE: Bullshit is all the reasons we give for living, and if we can't think up any reasons of our own, we always have the God bullshit . . .

Hunter's secretary whispered in awe, "Holy Mary, mother of Christ . . ."

Max spoke into the phone, "Yeah, what is it, Tom?"

BEALE: We don't know why the hell we're going through all this pointless pain, humiliation and decay, so there better be someone somewhere who does know; that's the God bullshit . . .

"He's saying life is bullshit," Max said, "and it is. So what're you screaming about?" He hung up the phone and it promptly rang again. Hunter's secretary picked it up.

BEALE: If you don't like the God bullshit, how about the man bullshit? Man is a noble creature who can order his own world. Who needs God?

"Mr. Amundsen for you, Mr. Schumacher," Hunter's secretary said.
"I'm not taking calls," Max said.

BEALE: Well, if there's anybody out there who can look around this demented slaughterhouse of a world we live in and tell me man is a noble creature, that man is full of bullshit. . . .

"I know he's sober," the director said to Hunter, "so he's got to be plain nuts." He giggled.
"What's so goddamn funny?" Hunter screamed.
"I can't help it, Harry, it's funny."

BEALE: I don't have any kids . . .

A phone rang and Hunter's secretary picked it up. Hunter turned to Max. "This is going out live to sixty-seven affiliates," he said.

"Leave him on," Max said.

BEALE: . . . and I was married for thirty-three years of shrill, shrieking fraud. . .

A breathless and distraught young woman burst into the control room. Seeing Max, she said, "Mr. Hackett's trying to get through to you."

"Tell Mr. Hackett to go fuck himself," Max said.

Upstairs, Diana Christensen was sitting alone watching Howard Beale on her office console.

BEALE: I don't have any bullshit left. I just ran out of it, you see . . .

Back in the control room, Frank Hackett and his assistant, Tom Cabell, wrenched the door open and strode in.

"Get him off!" Hackett roared. "Are you people nuts?"

The technical director tapped a button and the screen went to black.

Later, in Max's office, Hackett and Max screamed a great deal at each other while Howard Beale sat solemnly on the couch. Nelson Chaney occupied Max's desk and telephone. In the background there was a bedlam of executives as there had been after Beale's earlier broadcast.

Hackett was roaring. "The enormity of it! The

God bullshit! Oh, my God! We're going to take a bath for a million bucks tonight, you cockamamies! You Katzenjammer kids will never work in communications again!"

# CHAPTER 3

White-haired, patrician Edward Ruddy, chairman of the board, impeccably groomed, fastidious in a light topcoat, made his way through the crush of newspaper people, wire-service people, camera crews from CBS, NBC, ABC, from the local stations and more. A half dozen security guards were mustered to protect the elevators and they helped Ruddy get through the glaring camera lights and the horde of reporters thrusting mikes at him.

"I'm sorry," Ruddy said, "I don't have all the facts yet."

Upstairs on the twentieth floor, the top management floor, Max Schumacher stood in the deserted reception area. The decor was posh-austere, reflecting the eminence of the top executives whose offices were here. It was silent and empty now, cathedral-hushed. Down at the far end of the corridor, Nelson Chaney leaned through double doors and beckoned to Max. He started down the plush carpeting in response.

Max entered Ruddy's large, regal office. There were Impressionist originals on some of the walls. Through other walls of glass the grandeur of the New York skyline could be seen. Ruddy was sitting at his desk by now. John Wheeler, fifty-nine, silent, forceful, lounged in one of several leather chairs. Everybody nodded at everybody else and Max slumped into a leather chair.

Ruddy murmured to Chaney, "I'll want to see Mr. Beale after this."

Chaney picked up a phone and promptly called down to the fourteenth floor.

Ruddy said, "The way I hear it, Max, you're primarily responsible for this colossally stupid prank. Is that the fact?"

"That's the fact."

"It was unconscionable," Ruddy said. "There doesn't seem to be anything more to say."

"I have something to say, Ed. I'd like to know why that whole debasement of the News Division announced at the stockholders' meeting today was kept secret from me. You and I go back twenty years, Ed. I took this job with your personal assurance that you would back my autonomy against any encroachment. But ever since CCA acquired the UBS systems ten months ago, Hackett's been taking over everything. Who the hell's running this network, you or CCA? I mean, you're the chairman and Frank Hackett's just CCA's hatchet man. Nelson here—for Pete's sake, he's the president of the network—he hasn't got anything to say about anything any more. Who the hell's running this company, you or CCA?"

"I told you," Ruddy murmured, "at the stock-holders' meeting that we would discuss all that at our regular meeting tomorrow morning. If you had been patient, I would've explained to you that I too thought Frank Hackett precipitate and that the reorganization of the News Division would not be executed until everyone, especially you, Max, had been consulted and satisfied. Instead, you sulked off like a child and engaged this network in a shocking and disgraceful episode. Your position here is no longer tenable regard-less of how management is restructured. I ex-pect you to bring in your resignation at ten o'clock tomorrow morning and we will coordinate our statements to the least detriment of everyone."

Ruddy turned to Wheeler. "Bob McDonough will take over the News Division till we sort all this out." Then he spoke to Chaney. "I'd like to see Mr. Beale now."

Chaney was on the phone. "They're looking for him, Ed. They don't know where he is."

In the lobby of the UBS building, Howard Beale, bleached almost white by the glare of camera lights, almost totally obscured by the tidal crush of cameras, reporters, security guards around him, was saying, "Every day, five days a week, for fifteen years, I've been sitting behind that desk—the dispassionate pundit . . ."

Diana Christenson sat naked on her bed watch-ing Howard Beale's impromptu press conference on television.

BEALE: . . . Reporting with seemly detachment the daily parade of lunacies that constitute the news . . . and . . .

Also on the bed with Diana was a naked young stud who wasn't really interested in the 11:00 news. He was fondling, fingering, noddling and nuzzling Diana with the clear intention of mounting her.

BEALE: Just once I wanted to say what I really felt . . .

The stud was nibbling at Diana's breasts.
She watched the TV set with single-minded intensity. "Knock it off, Arthur," she said.

The next morning at nine o'clock Frank Hackett and Nelson Chaney were having an executive breakfast on a white-linened table. The office was Spartan, with Finnish chairs and a couch, the only decoration being the inevitable bank of four television monitors.

Chaney was saying, "Between national and local advertisers, Joe estimates well over half a million loss in revenue. Most of the affiliates who didn't carry the tape live took our cetaceans-in-the-Arctic filler, and the local advertisers, needless to say, screamed bloody murder. Most of them refuse to take make-goods; we'll simply have to refund . . ."

On the fourteenth floor, at nine-fifteen, Diana Christensen, stunning in a pants suit and carrying half a dozen scripts, briskly entered the door marked Department of Programming. Her secretary scurried after her just as Barbara Schlesinger came out of her own office carrying four scripts.

"Have you still got yesterday's overnights around?" Diana asked her secretary.

The woman nodded. "Shall I bring them in?"

"Yeah." Standing behind her desk, Diana scanned the front pages of the newspapers, then sat down to look over the overnight ratings on her desk. Her secretary entered with yesterday's overnights, gave them to Diana, who began to study them immediately. The secretary left as Barbara Schlesinger entered, sinking into a chair with a sigh.

"These are the four outlines submitted by Universal for an hour series," Barbara said. "You needn't bother to read them. I'll tell them to you. The first one is set in a large Eastern law school, presumably Harvard. The series is irresistibly entitled 'The New Lawyers.' The running characters are a crusty but benign ex-Supreme Court Justice, presumably Oliver Wendell Holmes by way of Dr. Zorba. There is a beautiful girl graduate student and the local district attorney who is brilliant but sometimes cuts corners . . ."

"Next," Diana said, studying the overnights.

"The second is called the 'Amazon Squad' . . ."

"Lady cops?"

"The running characters are a crusty but benign police lieutenant who's always getting heat from the commissioner, a hard-nosed, hard-drinking detective who thinks women belong in the kitchen and a brilliant and beautiful young girl cop fighting the feminist battle on the force . . ."

"We're up to our ears in lady cop shows," Diana said, studying the front page of the *Daily News*.

"The next one," Schlesinger said, "is another investigative reporter show. A crusty but benign managing editor who's always getting heat from the publisher . . ."

"You know," Diana said, "today is Yom Kippur, and they're worried about another war in the Middle East. They've discovered a blood clot in Nixon's right lung, there's a hurricane in Honduras, drought among the Tauregs, crop failure in India, two major banks have reduced their prime rate and—" she flipped the *Daily News* over so that Barbara could read it. "The whole front page of the *Daily News* is Howard Beale."

The newspaper showed a three-quarter page photo of the anchorman, topped by a 52-point headline which read: BEALE FIRED.

"It was also," Diana went on, "a two-column story on page one of the *Times*." She broke off to call her secretary. "Helen, call Mr. Hackett's office, see if he can give me a few minutes this morning."

At nine-thirty Max Schumacher and Bob McDonough entered the news room. It was a long, large windowless area, containing some forty desks, mostly unoccupied, a wire room, typewriters and banks of television monitors on the wall. At the moment, work had stopped and some sixty people, everyone in the news room—executives, secretaries, producers, assistant producers, head writers, writers, duty and assignment editors, desk assistants, artists, film and tape editors, reporters, newscasters, camera and audio men— all were gathered to hear Max Schumacher.

"Ladies and gentlemen," Max said, "I've been

at this network twelve years, and it's been on the whole a ball—"

Someone in the back yelled: "Louder!"

"And I want to thank you all," Max said more loudly. "Bob McDonough here will be taking over for me for the time being and, much as I hate to admit it, I'm sure everything will go along just fine without me . . ."

At ten o'clock Frank Hackett's secretary waved Diana into Hackett's office. He was sitting unhappily at his desk poring over memos from his affiliates department and reports from his sales department. He did not bother to look up as she came in.

"KTNS Kansas City refuses to carry our network news any more unless Beale is taken off the air."

Diana dropped a sheet of paper on Hackett's desk. "Did you see the overnights on the network news?" she asked. "It has an eight in New York and a nine in L.A. and a twenty-seven share in both cities. Last night, Howard Beale went on the air and yelled bullshit for two minutes and I can tell you right now that tonight's show will get a thirty share at least. I think we've lucked into something."

"Oh, for God's sake," Hackett said, "are you suggesting we put that lunatic back on the air yelling 'bullshit'?"

"Yes, I think we should put Beale back on the air tonight and keep him on. Did you see the *Times* this morning? Did you see the *News*? We've got press coverage on this you couldn't buy for a million dollars. Frank, that dumb show jumped five rating points in one night! Tonight's show has got to be at least fifteen! We just picked up twenty or thirty million people from Wednesday to Thursday! You're not going to get something like this dumped in your lap for the rest of your days, and you just can't piss it away! Howard Beale got up there last night and said what every American feels—that he's tired of all the bullshit. He's articulating the popular rage. I want that show, Frank. I can turn that show into the biggest smash in television."

"What do you mean, you want that show? It's a news show. It's not your department."

"I see Howard Beale as a latter-day prophet, a magnificent messianic figure, inveighing against the hyprocrisies of our times, a strip Savonarola, Monday through Friday. I tell you, Frank, that could just go through the roof. And I'm talking about a six-dollar-cost-per-thousand show! I'm talking about a hundred, a hundred-thirty-thousand-dollar minutes! Do you want to figure out the revenues of a strip show that sells for a hundred thousand bucks a minute? One show like that could pull this whole network right out of the hole! Now, Frank, it's being handed to us on a plate; let's not blow it!"

His intercom buzzed and he answered it. "Yes? Tell him I'll be a few more minutes." He clicked it off and turned to Diana. "Let me think it over."

"Frank," Diana said, "let's not go to committee about this. It's twenty after ten, and we want Beale in that studio by half-past six. We don't want to lose the momentum. . . ."

"For God's sake, Diana, we're talking about putting a manifestly irresponsible man on national television. I'd like to talk to Legal Affairs at least. And Herb Thackeray and certainly Joe Donnelly and Standards and Practices. And you know I'm going to be eyeball to eyeball with Mr. Ruddy on this. If I'm going to the mat with Ruddy, I want to make sure of some of my ground. I'm the one whose ass is going on the line. I'll get back to you, Diana."

At 12:20 five men sat at a table in the executive dining room. They were Frank Hackett, Nelson Chaney, Walter Amundsen, the general counsel for the network, Arthur Zangwill, vice-president for standards and practices, and Joe Donnelly, vice-president in charge of sales.

Nelson Chaney was standing. "I don't believe this!" he said. "I don't believe the top brass of a national television network are sitting around their Caesar salads . . ."

"The top brass of a *bankrupt* national television network," Frank Hackett said, "with projected losses of close to a hundred and fifty million dollars this year."

"I don't care how bankrupt," Chaney said. "You can't seriously be proposing, and the rest of us seriously considering, putting on a pornographic network news show! The FCC will kill us!"

"Sit down, Nelson," Hackett said. "The FCC can't do anything except rap our knuckles."

Chaney sat.

"I don't even want to think about the litigious possibilities, Frank," Walter Amundsen said. "We could be up to our ears in lawsuits."

"The affiliates won't carry it," Chaney said.

"The affiliates will kiss your ass if you can hand them a hit show," Hackett replied.

"The popular reaction . . ." said Chaney.

"We don't know the popular reaction," Hackett persisted, "that's what we have to find out."

"*The New York Times*—"

"*The New York Times* doesn't advertise on our network."

Chaney stood up again. "All I know is that this violates every canon of respectable broadcasting."

"We're not a respectable network," Hackett said. "We're a whorehouse network, and we have to take whatever we can get."

"Well I don't want any part of it," Chaney said. "I don't fancy myself the president of a whorehouse."

"That's very commendable of you, Nelson," Hackett said. "Now sit down and remember all those professions of high principle for your next appearance before the Senate Subcommittee on Communications. Your indignation has been duly recorded, you can always resign tomorrow." Again, Chaney sat.

"Mr. Ruddy—" Arthur Zangwill began.

Hackett interrupted. "We're not going to Mr. Ruddy about this. This is a network decision. Look, what in substance are we proposing? Merely to add editorial comment to our network news show. Brinkley, Sevareid and Reasoner all have their comments. So now Howard Beale will have his. I think we ought to give it a shot. Let's see what happens tonight."

"Well," Donnelly said, "I don't want to be the Babylonian messenger who has to tell Max Schumacher about this."

Hackett flagged a waiter. "Max Schumacher doesn't work at this network any more. Ruddy fired him last night." To the waiter, he said, "A telephone, please." Then he resumed. "Bob Mc-Donough's running the News Division."

A phone was placed before him and he picked it up. "Bob McDonough in news, please," Hackett said.

At 1:40 P.M. Max was in his office, talking on the phone and cleaning out his desk at the same time. Empty cartons were everywhere and he was dumping his files into boxes.

"I'm just fine, financially, Fred," Max said. "I cashed in my stock options back in April when CCA took over the network—" His other phone buzzed. "That's my other phone, Fred, thanks for calling." He hung up and picked up the other receiver.

"Max Schumacher. Hi, Dick. How's everything?"

Howard Beale walked in, carrying an eight-by-twelve photograph. Max looked up at him but continued with his conversation. "I don't know, Dick. I might teach, I might write a book, whatever the hell one does when one approaches the autumn of one's years."

Beale put the photograph on the desk in front of Max.

"My God, is that me? Was I ever that young?" He turned back to his call. "Howard just showed me a picture of the whole Ed Murrow gang when I was at CBS. My God, Bob Trout, Harry Reasoner, Cronkite, Hollenbeck, and that's you, Howard, right? I'll see you, Dick." He hung up.

"You remember this kid?" Howard Beale said. "He's the kid I think you once sent out to interview Cleveland Amory on vivisection."

Max began to shake with laughter. Milton Steinman poked his head in the office. "What the hell's so funny?" he asked.

An hour later, when Bob McDonough, interim head of the News Division, entered the executive offices, he saw a clot of people spilling out of Max Schumacher's office amid shouts of laughter. Even the secretaries had left their desks to join the fun. McDonough, wondering what the hell it was all about, made his way through the crush, murmuring, "Excuse me . . . sorry, honey, sorry."

What he saw was a room filled with news executives delightedly listening to a gang of middle-aged men remembering their maverick days.

"I jump out of bed in my pajamas," Max was saying, "I grab my raincoat, run down the stairs, run out into the middle of the street, flag a cab. I jump in, I yell: 'Take me to the middle of the George Washington Bridge!'"

There was a howl of laughter.

"The driver turns around and he says, 'Don't do it, kid, you got your whole life ahead of you!'"

The room rocked with laughter and when it subsided, Bob McDonough spoke from the doorway. "Well, if you think that's funny, wait'll you hear this. I've just come down from Frank Hackett's office and he wants to put Howard back on the air tonight. Apparently the ratings jumped five points last night, and he wants Howard to go back on and do his angry-man thing."

"What are you talking about?" Steinman asked.

"I'm telling you—they want Howard to go on denouncing bullshit. They want Howard to go on spontaneously letting out his anger, a latter-day prophet inveighing against the hypocrisies of our times."

"Hey, that sounds pretty good," Howard Beale said.

"Who's this they?" Max asked.

"Hackett," McDonough said. "Chaney was there. the Legal Affairs guy, and that girl from programming."

"Christenson?" Max said. "What's she got to do with it?"

"You're kiding, aren't you, Bob?" Gianini said.

"I'm not kidding. I told them: 'We're running a news department down there, not a circus. And Howard Beale isn't a bearded lady. And if you think I'll go along with this bastardization of the news, you can have my resignation along with Max Schumacher's right now. And I think I'm speaking for Howard Beale and everybody else down there in news.'"

"Hold it, McDonough, that's my job you're turning down," Beale said. "I'll go nuts without some kind of work. What's wrong with being an angry prophet denouncing the hypocrisies of our times? What do you think, Max?"

"Do you *want* to be an angry prophet denouncing the hypocrisies of our times?"

"Yeah, I think I'd *like* to be an angry prophet denouncing the hypocrisies of our times."

"Then grab it," Max said.

At three o'clock, Edward Ruddy, slim, slight, imperially elegant in banker's gray, approached room 509. Secretaries and others who encountered him looked surprised, but offered only polite "Good afternoons." He entered Max's office and closed the door.

51

"Nelson Chaney tells me Beale may actually go on the air this evening," Ruddy said.

"As far as I know, Howard's going to do it," Max said. "Are you going to sit still for this, Ed?"

Ruddy took a folded piece of paper from his inside jacket pocket. "Yes. I think Hackett's overstepped himself. There's some kind of corporate maneuvering going on, Max. Hackett is clearly forcing a confrontation. That would account for his behavior at the stockholders' meeting. However, I think he's making a serious mistake with this Beale business. CCA would never make such an open act of brigandage, especially against the News Division. They are specifically enjoined from any manipulation of the News Division in the articles of acquisition. I suspect CCA will be upset by Hackett's presumptuousness; certainly Mr. Jensen will. So I'm going to let Hackett have his head for a while. He just might lose it over this Beale business." He laid the piece of paper on Max's desk.

"I'd like you to reconsider your resignation," Ruddy said, moving to the couch and crossing his legs. "I have to assume Hackett wouldn't take such steps without some support on the CCA board. I'll have to go directly to Mr. Jensen. When that happens I'm going to need every friend I've got. And I certainly don't want Hackett's people in all the divisional positions. So I'd like you to stay on, Max."

"Of course."

Ruddy stood. "Thank you, Max." Then he left.

That was on Thursday. On the following Monday at 7:00 P.M., Max sat alone in his office watching the Howard Beale show. On the previous Thursday and Friday the show had had a 14 rating and a 37 share, very good for a news program. Clearly, the audience was curious. But on the whole, Howard Beale played his role of mad prophet poorly. He was uncertain, sometimes inaudible, manifestly uncomfortable. The press, without exception, was hostile and industry reaction was negative.

Max clicked off the set as the news show came to an end. He sat quietly with his hands folded on his desk, glumly regarding his fingers. After a moment, he became aware of another presence and looked to the doorway where Diana Christensen was standing, wearing a white blouse, dark slacks and carrying her jacket and purse. Framed in the doorway, backlit by the lights of the deserted common room, she appeared sensuous, even voluptuous.

"Did you know," she said, as she entered his office, "there are a number of psychics working as licensed brokers on Wall Street?" She sat down and fished a cigarette from her purse.

"Some of them," Diana went on, "counsel their clients by use of Tarot cards. They're all pretty successful, even in a bear market and selling short. I met one of them a couple of weeks ago and thought of doing a show around her—the Wayward Witch of Wall Street, something like that. But of course, if her tips were any good, she could wreck the market. So I called her this morning and asked her how she was on predicting the future. She said she was occasionally prescient. 'For example,' she said, 'I just had a fleeting vision of you sitting in an office with a craggy middle-aged man with whom you are or will be emotionally involved.' And here I am."

"She does all this with Tarot cards?" Max said.

"No, this one operates on parapsychology. She has trance-like episodes and feels things in her energy field. I think this lady can be very useful to you, Max."

"In what way?"

"Well, you put on news shows, and here's someone who can predict tomorrow's news for you. Her name, aptly enough, is Sybil. Sybil the Soothsayer. You could give her two minutes of trance at the end of the Howard Beale show, say once a week, Friday, which is suggestively occult, and she could oraculate. Then next week, everyone tunes in to see how good her predictions were."

"Maybe she could do the weather," Max said.

Diana smiled. "Your network news show is going to need some spiking, Max, if it's going to hold. Beale's angry-man thing will wear thin soon. He's too kvetchy. I think you should take on a comedy writer to punch up his jokes." She paused. "I see you don't fancy my suggestions."

"Hell," Max said, "you're not being serious, are you?"

"Oh, I'm serious. The fact is, I could make your Beale show the highest-rated news show in television if you'd let me have a crack at it."

"What do you mean, have a crack at it?"

"I'd like to program it for you, develop it. I wouldn't interfere with the actual news. But TV is show biz, Max, and even the news has to have a little showmanship."

"My God," Max said, "you *are* serious."

"I watched your six o'clock news today. It's

straight tabloid. You had a minute and a half on that lady riding a bike naked in Central Park. On the other hand, you had less than a minute of hard national and international news. It was all sex, scandal, brutal crimes, sports, lost puppies and children with incurable diseases. So I don't think I'll listen to any protestations of high standards of journalism. You're right down in the street soliciting audiences like the rest of us. All I'm saying is, if you're going to hustle, at least do it right. I'm going to bring this up at tomorrow's network meeting, but I don't like network hassles. I was hoping you and I could work this out between us. That's why I'm here now."

Max sighed. "I was hoping you were looking for an emotional involvement with a craggy middle-aged man."

"I wouldn't rule that out entirely," Diana said. They appraised each other for a moment. Clearly there were possibilities for something more than a professional relationship.

"Well, Diana," Max said, "you bring all your ideas up at the meeting tomorrow. Because if you don't, I will. I think Howard is making a goddamn fool of himself and so does everybody Howard and I know in this industry. So tomorrow Howard goes back to the old format and this gutter depravity comes to an end."

Diana smiled and got to her feet. "Okay." She leaned forward to flick ashes into his ashtray. Half-shaded by the cone of light from his desk lamp, it was clear that she was bra-less and Max noted the assertive swells of her body. She moved languidly to the door as Max spoke again.

"I don't get it, Diana. You hung around till

half-past seven and came all the way down here just to pitch a couple of looney show-biz ideas when you knew goddamn well I'd laugh you out of this office. I don't get it. What's your scam in this anyway?"

She walked back to his desk and crushed her cigarette out. "Max, I don't know why you suddenly changed your mind about resigning, but I do know Hackett's going to throw you out on your ass in January. My little visit here tonight was just a courtesy made out of respect for your stature in the industry and because I've personally admired you ever since I was a kid majoring in speech at the University of Missouri. But sooner or later, now or in January, with or without you, I'm going to take over your network news show and I figured I might as well start tonight."

"I think I once gave a lecture at the University of Missouri," Max said.

"I was in the audience. I had a terrible schoolgirl crush on you for a couple of months." She smiled and headed for the doorway again.

"Listen," Max said, "if we can get back for a moment to that gypsy who predicted all that about emotional involvements and middle-aged men: what're you doing for dinner tonight?"

Diana paused and then moved briskly back to the desk, picked up the phone and tapped out a number. Then she spoke. "I can't make it tonight, luv, call me tomorrow." She put the phone back and looked Max in the eye.

"Do you have a favorite restaurant?" he asked.

"I eat anything," Diana said.

"Son of a bitch. I get the feeling I'm being made."

"You sure are."

"I better warn you," Max said, "I don't do anything on the first date."

"We'll see."

As she moved to the door, Max stared down at his desk and muttered to himself, "Schmuck, what're you getting into?"

Two hours later, Diana was finishing her ice cream while Max flagged a waiter for coffee.

"You're married, surely," she said.

"Twenty-six years. I have a married daughter in Seattle who's six months' pregnant, and a younger girl who starts at Northwestern in January."

"Well, Max, here we are—middle-aged man reaffirming his middle-aged manhood and terrified young woman with a father complex. What sort of script do you think we can make out of this?"

"Terrified, are you?"

She regarded him affably. "Terrified out of my skull, man. I'm the hip generation, man, right on, cool, groovy, remember all that? Letting it all hang out, do-your-own-thing, getting it all together, expansion of the soul, cool, man. God, what frauds we were. In my first year at college, I lived in a commune, dropped acid daily, joined four radical groups and fucked myself silly on a bare wooden floor while somebody chanted Sufi suras. I lost six weeks of my sophomore year because they put me away for trying to jump off the top floor of the administration building. I've been on the top floor ever since. Don't open any windows around me because I might just jump out. Am I scaring you off?"

"No."

"I was married for four years," she continued, "and pretended to be happy and had six years of analysis and pretended to be sane. My husband ran off with his boyfriend, and I had an affair with my analyst. He told me I was the worst lay he ever had. I can't tell you how many men have told we what a lousy lay I am. I apparently have a masculine temperament. I arouse quickly, consummate prematurely, and can't wait to get my clothes back on and get out of that bedroom. I seem to be inept at everything except my work. I'm goddamn good at my work and so I confine myself to that. All I want out of life is a thirty share and a twenty rating."

"The corridor gossip says you're Frank Hackett's back-stage girl."

"I'm not." She smiled. "Frank's a corporation man, body and soul. He surrendered his spirit to CCA years ago. He's a marketing-merchandising-management machine, precision-tooled for corporate success. He's married to one CCA board member's daughter, he attends another board member's church, his children aged two and five are already enrolled in a third member's alma mater. He has no loves, lusts or allegiances that are not consummately directed towards becoming a CCA board member himself. So why should he fuck around with me? I'm not even a stockholder."

"How about your loves, lusts and allegiances?"

They smiled at each other.

"Is your wife in town?" she asked.

"Yes."

"Well, then, we better go to my place."

Max and Diana lay naked in the dark. Both were still breathless from having made love violently.

"Wow," Diana said, "and you were the guy who kept telling me how he was going to be a grandfather in three months."

"Hell," he said, "you were the girl who kept telling me what a lousy lay she was."

She got out of bed and stood naked in the darkness, arms akimbo, looking happily down at Max on the bed.

"All right, enough of this lovemaking. Are you going to let me take over your network news show or not?"

Max laughed. "Forget it. Tomorrow, Howard Beale goes back to being a straight anchorman. I'll tell him first thing in the morning."

In his own bedroom Howard Beale lay fast asleep. Suddenly, he got up on one elbow, eyes still closed, cocking his head as if he were listening to someone mumbling from the rocking chair across the room.

"I can't hear you," he said. "You'll have to speak a little louder."

He paused, then said, "You're kidding. How the hell would I know what the truth is?"

He sat up fully, got out of bed, walked around and stared at the empty rocker, nodding his head as if following a complicated argument.

"What the hell is this, the burning bush? For God's sake, I'm not Moses—"

Whoever he thought he was talking to apparently got up and crossed the room to an overstuffed chair, since Howard followed the movement with his eyes. Finally, he moved to the side of his bed and perched there in order to continue the curious conversation.

"Why me? I'm a deteriorating old man."

He listened, sighed and shrugged.

"Okay," he said.

# CHAPTER 4

Max entered the news room at nine o'clock the next day. It was a bright, sunny morning and the room hummed with its usual activity. Harry Hunter was going over some wire releases with his head writer and looked up as Max approached.

"Howard in his office?" Max asked. Hunter nodded.

"Harry, I'm killing this whole screwball angry prophet thing. We're going back to straight news as of tonight's show."

"Okay," Hunter said.

Max veered off for Howard's office. He found Howard at his typewriter.

"Howard," Max said, "we're going back to straight news tonight. You don't have to be the mad prophet any more."

Howard turned around with a sweet smile. "I

must go on with what I'm doing," he said. "I have been called. This is my witness and I must make it."

This gave Max pause, to say the least.

"You must make what, Howard?"

"I must make my witness. I must lead the people from the waters. I must stay their stampede to the sea."

Max stepped inside the office and closed the door.

"You must stay their what, Howard?"

"I must stay their headlong suicidal stampede to the sea."

Max regarded Howard for a moment. "Well, hallelujah, are you putting me on or have you flipped or what?"

"I have heard voices, Max," Howard said serenely.

"You have heard voices. Swell. What kind of voices, Howard? Still small voices in the night or the mighty thunder of God? Howard, you've finally done it. You've gone over the edge. You're nuts."

"I have been called. This is my witness, and I must make it."

"Not on my goddamn network news show," Max said, and he left the office to go back into the news room.

He approached Harry Hunter who was muttering away to Milton Steinman in the doorway of Hunter's office.

"Can I see you guys a minute?" Max said, leading the way into Hunter's office. He closed the door and regarded the two men. "Listen, did either of you guys talk to Howard this morning?"

"Sure," Hunter said.

"Did he seem a little odd to you? Because I just went in to tell him we were going back to the old format, and he said he has been hearing voices and he has to save the people from the waters."

"He's been an absolute doll the last couple of days," Hunter said, "and I'll tell you this—he hasn't hit the booze in a week."

"You haven't noticed anything screwy about him? Like remember last year, he cracked up when his wife died? Maybe he's putting me on because he kept saying he's been hearing voices and he has to make his witness."

"Sounds like he's putting you on," Steinman said.

"Max, I'm not so sure we ought to go back to the old format," Hunter said. "I think we ought to let Howard go on with this angry prophet thing. I got to admit I look forward to his outbursts. And my kids love it."

"Your kids love it," Max said. "Swell."

"My kids never watched a news show in their lives," Steinman said, "but last night my wife had to hold dinner because they had a whole bunch of their friends in to see Howard Beale. Joe Donnelly says his kids watch too. Joe says we might be tapping a rich consumer vein with Howard, put a dent in the teen-age market—"

"I don't give a damn about dents in the teen-age market," Max said. "I said we're going back to the old format, and we're going back to the old format."

"Okay, okay."

Max strode out of the office and started to cross the news room but he paused again outside Howard Beale's door. "You all right, Howard?" he asked.

Howard turned from his typewriter to regard Max with a beatific smile.

"I'm beautiful."

"Now, stop the shit, Howard. I'm not kidding around about this. You go back to straight anchorman tonight. I'm the voice you're hearing now, and this voice is telling you we're doing a straight news show from now on. Okay?"

Howard turned away and resumed pecking away at his typewriter. Max frowned and stepped back into the news room where Harry Hunter and Milton Steinman were waiting for him.

"I don't think he's putting me on," Max said. "I think he's flipped. Keep an eye on him." He moved off.

At 6:29 P.M. the control room staff were all at their posts, murmuring. Harry Hunter was on the phone.

"Max," he muttered, "I'm telling you he's fine. He's been sharp all day, he's been funny as hell. He had everybody cracking up at the rundown meeting. I told him, I told him. . . ."

On the show monitor Howard Beale could be seen at his desk, shuffling papers, looking up for his cue. The wall clock clicked to 6:30. The director murmured into his mike. Howard looked out from the screen to his vast audience and said:

BEALE: Last night, I was awakened from a fitful sleep at shortly after two o'clock in the morning by a shrill, sibilant, faceless Voice that was sitting in my rocking chair. I couldn't make it out at first in the dark bedroom. I said: "I'm sorry, you'll have to talk a little louder." And the Voice said to me: "I want you to tell the people the truth, not an easy thing to do; because the people don't want to know the truth." I said: "You're kidding. How the hell would I know what the truth is?" I mean, you have to picture me sitting there at the foot of the bed talking to an empty rocking chair. I said to myself: "Howard, you are some kind of a banjo-brain sitting here talking to an empty chair." But the Voice said to me: "Don't worry about the truth. I'll put the words in your mouth." And I said: "What is this, the burning bush? For God's sake, I'm not Moses." And the Voice said to me: "And I'm not God, what's that got to do with it?"

Harry Hunter, still on the phone, sat as the other control room staff did, staring at Howard Beale on monitor.

"What do you want me to do?" he asked.

Max, in his office, chin in hand, phone at his ear, stared glumly at Howard on his console.

"Nothing," Max said.

BEALE: And the Voice said to me: "We're not talking about eternal truth, absolute truth or ultimate truth! We're talking about impermanent, transient, human truth! I don't expect you people to be capable of truth! But goddamnit, you're at least capable of self-preservation! That's good enough! I want you to go out and tell the people to preserve themselves."

"Right now," Max muttered on the phone, "I'm trying to remember the name of that psychiatrist that took care of him when his wife died."

BEALE: And I said to the Voice: "Why me?" And the Voice said: "Because you're on television, dummy!"

Diana was watching Howard on her office console.
"Beautiful!" she said.

BEALE: "Right now, you've got forty million Americans listening to you, and after tonight's show you'll have fifty million. For Pete's sake, I don't expect you to walk the land in sackcloth and ashes preaching Armageddon. You're on TV, man!"

Max had hung up the phone and was leafing through a loose-leaf address book.

BEALE: So I thought about it for a moment . . .

Max tapped out a telephone number on his private line.

BEALE: . . . and then I said: "Okay."

"Doctor Sindell?" Max said. "My name is Max Schumacher, I'm at United Broadcasting Systems, and I hope you remember me. I'm a friend of Howard Beale, whom you treated for a few months last year . . ."

A short time later, Howard Beale and Harry Hunter, followed by the rest of the control room staff, entered the news room. Howard, walking ramrod straight, eyes uplifted, serene to the point of beatitude, accompanied Hunter into his— Howard's—office. They found Max sitting on the couch. He stood when they entered and said, "Close the door, Harry." Harry did.

"Sit down, Howard," Max continued. "I'm taking you off the air. I called your psychiatrist."

Howard sat serenely behind his desk. "What's happening to me, Max, isn't mensurate in psychiatric terms."

"I think you're having a breakdown," Max said. "You require treatment and Dr. Sindell agrees."

"This is not a psychotic episode. It is a cleansing moment of clarity. I don't expect you or Dr. Sindell to understand so nonmolecular a thing as a state of grace, but that is what I am in right now, and all I ask of you is that you accept it without understanding." He stood up.

"I am imbued, Max. I am imbued with some special spirit. It's not a religious feeling, it is a shocking eruption of great electrical energy! I feel vivid and flashing as if suddenly I had been plugged into some great cosmic electromagnetic field. I feel connected to all living things, to flowers, birds, to all the animals of the world and even to some great unseen living force, what

I think the Hindus call prana." He stood rigidly erect, his eyes staring mindlessly out, his face revealing the strain of so transcendental a state.

"It is not a breakdown. I have never felt so ordered in my life! It is a shattering and beautiful sensation! It is the exalted flow of the space-time continuum, save that it is spaceless and timeless and of such loveliness! I feel on the verge of some great ultimate truth." He stared haggardly at Max, his breath coming with great difficulty now. He shouted.

"You will not take me off the air for now or for any other spaceless time!" Then he promptly fell into a dead swoon on the floor.

Max hurried to his friend's prostrate form. "Jesus Christ," he said.

"Is he okay?" Hunter asked from the door.

"He's breathing anyway," Max said, bending over Howard. "I'll have to take him to my house again for the night."

While Max and his wife were fast asleep in their hushed room, a thunderstorm crashed outside the apartment. Rain pelted against the windows. In the living room, dark, hushed, Howard was asleep on the couch. Or rather, he had been asleep, for now he slowly sat up, then stood in his borrowed pajamas, went to the hall closet, fetched a raincoat, unchained and unbolted the door and went out.

At 7:30 the following morning thunder was still rumbling and rain was slashing through the streets. The sky was dark and lowering. An alarm clock buzzed in Max's bedroom and Louise Schumacher, a handsome matron of fifty, clicked it off and got out of bed. Max turned in the bed and slept on. Louise listened to the rain and thunder, started sleepily for the bathroom, paused and then went to the back hallway and into the living room.

There she stood, frowning. The couch, which had been made up for a bed, had clearly been slept in but was now empty. She looked back up the hallway to the guest bathroom. The door was open and there was obviously no one inside. She padded across the living room-dining room area and poked her head into the kitchen, then went back to the back hallway, pausing a moment outside her daughter's closed bedroom door. She opened it, looked in, closed it and then returned to her own bedroom. She sat on Max's side of the bed and shook him awake.

"Wake up, Max. Howard's gone. I'll make you some coffee."

Max muttered, "Shit." Then he slowly sat up.

Frank Hackett's office was filled with Diana Christensen, Herb Thackeray and Max, slumped on a soft chair. Hackett was in a rage, shouting at him.

"What do you mean, you don't know where he is? The son of a bitch is a hit, goddamnit! Over two thousand phone calls! Go down to the mailroom! As of this minute, over fourteen thousand telegrams! The response is sensational! Herb, tell him—"

Herb Thackeray started to open his mouth but Hackett interrupted. "Herb's phone hasn't stopped ringing! Every goddamn affiliate from Albuquerque to Sandusky! The response is sensational!" His phone rang and he seized it.

"What? . . . All right . . ." He hung up and snapped at Thackeray. "It's your office, Herb. You better get back there."

Hackett roared on as Thackeray left. "Moldanian called me! Joe Donnelly called me! We've got a goddamn hit, a goddamn hit! Diana, show him the *Times!* We even got an editorial in the holy goddamn *New York Times*. 'A Call to Morality!' That crazy son of a bitch Beale has caught on! So don't tell me you don't know where he is!"

Max roared back. "I don't know where he is! He may be jumping off a roof for all I know. The man is insane. He's no longer responsible for himself. He needs care and treatment. And all you graverobbers care about is that he's a hit!"

"You know, Max," Diana said, "it's just possible that he isn't insane, that he is, in fact, imbued with some special spirit."

"Oh Jesus," Max said.

"Jesus for one. There have been charismatic men before, men who have come forth in times of great meanness of spirit to lead the people . . ."

"Holy Moses!"

"Moses for another," Diana said. "Saint Joan, Gandhi, and I'm sure all of them were considered nuts in their time."

"My God, I'm supposed to be the romantic; you're supposed to be the hard-bitten realist."

"All right. Howard Beale obviously fills a void. The audience out there obviously wants a prophet, even a manufactured one, even if he's mad as Moses. By tomorrow, he'll have a fifty share, maybe even a sixty share. Howard Beale is processed instant God, and right now it looks like he may just go over bigger than Mary Tyler Moore."

"I'm not putting Howard back on the air," Max said.

"It's not your show any more, Max, it's mine," she said.

"You're nuts. You're nuttier than Howard."

"I gave her the show, Schumacher," Hackett said. "I'm putting the network news show under programming. Mr. Ruddy has had a mild heart attack and is not taking calls. In his absence, I'm making all network decisions, including one I've been wanting to make a long time: you're fired. I want you out of this building by noon. I'll leave word with the security guards to throw you out if you're still here."

"Well, let's just say, fuck you, Hackett," Max said. "You want me out you're going to have to drag me out kicking and screaming. And the whole News Division will walk out kicking and screaming with me."

"You think they're going to quit their jobs for you? Not in this depression, buddy."

"When Ruddy gets back, he'll have your ass."

"I got a hit, Schumacher, and Ruddy doesn't count any more. He was hoping I'd fall on my face with this Beale show but I didn't. It's a big, fat, big-titted hit, and I don't have to waffle around with Ruddy any more. If he wants to take me up before the CCA board, let him. All they know at CCA is they've got a network that's in the shithouse for a hundred and three million dollars, and I'm going to hand them this demented Howard Beale show that's going to put this network into profit. Do you think Ruddy's stupid enough to go to the CCA board and say: 'I'm taking our one hit show off the air'? And comes November 14, I'm going to be standing up there at the annual CCA management review meeting, and I'm going to announce projected earnings for this network for the first time in five years. And believe me, Mr. Jensen will be sitting there rocking back and forth in his little chair, and he's going to say: 'That's very good, Frank, keep it up.' So don't have any illusions about who's running this network from now on. You're fired. I want you out of your office before noon or I'll have you thrown out."

Max turned to Diana. "And you go along with this?"

"Well, Max, I told you I didn't want a network hassle over this. I told you I'd much rather work the Beale show out just between the two of us."

Max stood. "Well, let's just say, fuck you too, honey." He turned to Hackett. "Howard Beale may be my best friend! I'll go to court. I'll put him in a hospital before I let you exploit him like a carnival freak."

"You get your psychiatrists," Hackett said, "and I'll get mine."

Max headed for the door. "I'm going to spread this whole reeking business in every paper and on every network, independent, group and affiliated station in this country. I'm going to make a lot of noise about this."

"Great," Hackett said, "we need all the press we can get."

Max left. Hackett clicked on his intercom. "Get me Mr. Cabell," he said. Then he turned to

Diana. "Something going on between you and Schumacher?"

"Not any more," she sighed.

"Tom," Hackett said, "Howard Beale has disappeared. Tell Harriman to prepare a statement for the news media. And call the cops and tell them to find the crazy son of a bitch."

At 6:40 that night it was still raining. Rain lashed the street and pedestrians struggled against the slashing torrents. Howard Beale, drenched, wearing a coat over his pajamas, his gray hair plastered in streaks to his brow, hunched against the rain, climbed the steps and pushed through the glass doors of the UBS building.

"How do you do, Mr. Beale," a security guard said.

Howard stared haggardly at the guard and said, "I have to make my witness."

"Sure thing, Mr. Beale," said the affable security man.

Beale plodded off to the elevators.

In the news control room Diana Christenson stood in the back as Jack Snowden, Beale's replacement, was reading the news—straight, without prophecies or side comments. Snowden could be seen on the monitor.

SNOWDEN: The vice-president-designate was on the road today and stopped off in Provo, Utah, and in a speech in the basketball arena at Brigham Young University . . .

The production assistant said, "Five seconds . . ."

"Twenty-five in Provo . . ." said the technical director.

"And . . . two . . ." the director said.

SNOWDEN: Mr. Rockefeller had some strong words to say about the Arab oil producing nations. More on that story from Edward Fletcher. . . .

Harry Hunter answered a buzz on his phone. "Yeah? Okay." He hung up and turned to Diana. "He came in the building about five minutes ago."

"Get ready to roll her," the director said.

"Ten seconds coming to one . . ." said the production assistant.

Harry turned to the director, "Did you get that, Gene?"

The director nodded and passed instructions on to his assistant on the studio floor. On the show monitor they could see footage of Rockefeller crowding his way to the speaker's rostrum and over that image, the voice of Edward Fletcher in Provo, Utah.

FLETCHER: This was Rockefeller's first public appearance since he was named vice-president-designate, and he spoke sharply about inflation and high Arab oil prices . . .

On the show monitor Rockefeller flipped onto the screen.

ROCKEFELLER: Perhaps the most dramatic evidence of the political impact on inflation is the action by the OPEC countries and the

Arab oil countries in arbitrarily raising the price of oil four hundred percent . . .

Nobody in the control room was paying too much attention to Nelson Rockefeller; all were watching the double bank of black-and-white monitors which showed Howard Beale entering the studio, drenched, hunched, staring gauntly off into his own space, moving with single-minded purpose across the studio floor past cameras and cables and nervous cameramen, sound men, electricians, assistant directors and associate producers to his desk which was being vacated by Jack Snowden. On the show monitor the film clip of Rockefeller ended.

"And one . . ." the director said.

Suddenly, the obsessed face of Howard Beale, gaunt, haggard, red-eyed with unworldly fervor, hair streaked and plastered on his brow, filled the monitor screen.

BEALE: I don't have to tell you things are bad. Everybody knows things are bad. It's a depression. Everybody's out of work or scared of losing their job, the dollar buys a nickel's worth, banks are going bust, shopkeepers keep a gun under the counter, punks are running wild in the streets, and there's nobody anywhere who seems to know what to do, and there's no end to it. We know the air's unfit to breathe and our food is unfit to eat, and we sit and watch our TVs while some local newscaster tells us today we had fifteen homicides and sixty-three violent crimes, as if that's the way it's supposed to be. We all know things are bad. Worse than bad. They're crazy. It's like everything's going crazy. So we don't go out any more. We sit in the house and slowly the world we live in gets smaller, and all we ask is please, at least, leave us alone in our own living rooms. Let me have my toaster and my TV and my hair-dryer and my steel-belted radials, and I won't say anything, just leave us alone. Well, I'm not going to leave you alone. I want you to get mad. I don't want you to riot. I don't want you to protest. I don't want you to write your congressman. Because I wouldn't know what to tell you to write. I don't know what to do about the depression and the inflation and the defense budget and the Russians and crime in the street. All I know is first you got to get mad. You've got to say: "I'm a human being, goddamnit. My life has value." I want you to get out of your chairs and go to the window. Right now. I want you to go to the window, open it, and stick your head out and yell. I want you to yell: *"I'm mad as hell and I'm not going to take this any more!"*

Diana grabbed Hunter's shoulder. "How many stations does this go out live to?"

"Sixty-seven," he said. "I think it goes out to Atlanta and Louisville, I think. . . ."

BEALE: Get up from your chairs. Go to the window. Open it. Stick your head out and yell and keep yelling.

Diana was on her way out of the control room, scurrying down a corridor and looking for a phone. Picking up the receiver, she said, "Give me Station Relations . . . Herb, this is Diana Christensen. Are you watching? Because I want you to call every affiliate carrying this live. . . . I'll be right up."

She hung up, got into an elevator and rode to the fifteenth floor. Bursting out of the elevator, she strode down the corridor to where a clot of executives and office personnel blocked an open doorway. She pushed through into Herb Thackeray's office. He was on the phone staring up at Howard Beale on his wall monitor.

BEALE: First, you have to get mad. When you're mad enough . . .

Both Thackeray's office and his secretary's office were filled with people. Diana shouted at him, "Who are you talking to?"

"WCGG, Atlanta," he said.

"Are they yelling in Atlanta?" she asked.

BEALE: . . . we'll figure out what to do about the depression. . . .

Thackeray spoke into the phone, "Are they yelling in Atlanta, Ted?"

In Atlanta, the general manager of WCGG, a portly fifty-eight-year-old man, stood by his open window and stared out into the gathering dusk, holding his phone. From far off across the foliage surrounding his suburban station he could hear a faint rumble.

"Herb," he said into his phone, "so help me, I think they're yelling."

In Thackeray's office a man popped his head in and said, "They're yelling in Baton Rouge."

BEALE: Things have got to change. But you can't change unless you're mad. You have to get mad. Go to the window . . .

Diana, who had been listening to the people yelling in Baton Rouge, gave the phone back to Thackeray's assistant. "Next time somebody asks you to explain what ratings are, you tell them: that's ratings!" She exulted. "Son of a bitch, we struck the mother lode!"

In Max Schumacher's apartment, Max, Louise and their seventeen-year-old daughter, Caroline, were watching the news show in their living room.

BEALE: . . . stick your head out and yell. I want you to yell: *"I'm mad as hell and I'm not going to take this any more!"*

Caroline got up from her chair and headed for the living-room window.

"Where are you going?" her mother asked.

"I want to see if anybody's yelling," Caroline said.

BEALE: Right now. Get up. Go to your window . . .

Caroline opened the window and looked out on the rain-swept streets of the upper East Side, with its huge, anonymous apartment houses and occasional brownstones. It was very dark; a distant clap of thunder crashed somewhere and lightning shattered the darkness. In the sudden hush following the thunder, a thin voice down the block could be heard shouting: "I'm mad as hell and I'm not going to take this any more!"

BEALE: Open your window . . .

Max joined his daughter, rain spraying against his face. He saw occasional windows open and just across from his apartment house, a man opened the front door of a brownstone. "I'm mad as hell," the man shouted, "and I'm not going to take this any more!"

Other shouts could be heard. From his twenty-third-floor vantage point, Max saw the erratic landscape of Manhattan buildings for some blocks, and silhouetted heads in window after window, here, there, and then seemingly everywhere, shouting out into the slashing black rain of the streets:

*"I'm mad as hell and I'm not going to take this any more!"*

A terrifying enormous clap of natural thunder was followed by a frantic jagged flash of lightning and now the gathering chorus of scattered shouts seemed to be coming from the whole huddled horde of the city's people, screaming together in fury, an indistinguishable tidal roar of human rage as formidable as the natural thunder roaring, thundering, rumbling above. It sounded like a Nuremberg rally; the air trembled from the noise of it.

# NETWORK

Max stood with his daughter by the open terrace window-doors, rain spraying against them, listening to the stupefying sounds. He closed his eyes and sighed. There was nothing he could do about it any more; it was out of his hands.

# CHAPTER 5

By mid-October, "The Howard Beale Show," had settled in at a 42 share, more than equalling all the other network news shows combined.

In the September rating book "The Howard Beale Show" was listed as the fourth highest rated show of the month, surpassed only by "All in the Family," "Rhoda" and "Chico and the Man." It was a phenomenal state of affairs for a news program. "The Howard Beale Show" was the hottest thing to hit network television in anyone's memory.

On October 16, Diana Christensen flew to Los Angeles for what the trade calls powwows and confabs with her West Coast programming executives.

At a luncheon-business meeting Diana sat with Glenn Kossoff and Barbara Schlesinger; the head of the story department, West Coast; a man from Audience Research; and a woman who was vice-president of daytime programming, West Coast. They all sat around a mod-shaped conference table except for Diana, who was moving toward a large display board at the far end of the table. It stretched the length of the wall and was an improvised programming board. It showed, through moveable heavy cardboard pieces, what all four networks were showing by the half hour, for all seven days of the week.

"Next September," Diana said, "I want Wednesday night to be all UBS. I'll tell you now—we're going to expand 'The Howard Beale Show' to an hour in January, which'll give us a hell of a lead-in to eight o'clock. On Wednesday nights, I want to follow that with two strong hours, no sit-coms, nothing lightweight."

Bill Herron poked his head into the room. He said to Diana, "I've got Laureen Hobbs's lawyer on the phone. Is five-thirty okay, and where would you like to meet, here or at the hotel?"

Diana turned to Schlesinger, "Is five-thirty okay?"

"You've got Quinn Martin at five."

"Let's see Hy Norman at five," Diana said, "and see if Quinn can come in at two-thirty."

"Don't forget you've got dinner with the Legal Affairs people at eight," Schlesinger said.

Diana nodded to Herron. "Five-thirty is fine, and at my office, if they don't mind." She turned back at her board and resumed her exhortation.

"What I want right now are 'Movies of the Week' we can use for pilots. I want five 'Movies of the Week' ready by March at the outside, preferably sooner. I want to come in September with two powerhouse hour shows to follow the Beale show on Wednesday night."

Later that afternoon, Diana sat in an utterly bland office kept for visiting firemen. She was behind the desk, Barbara Schlesinger was on the couch, as Glen Kossoff, ushering two gentlemen out, spotted someone in the outer office. "Hi," he said, "come on in."

He motioned to a silver-haired, suntanned, fresh-from-the-tennis-court man dressed in California elegance, rakish blazer, an archtype of all L.A. television packagers. He was Hy Norman.

"Hy, I think you know Barbara Schlesinger, but I don't know if you know Diana Christensen."

Sinking casually into the visitor's chair, crossing his legs, flashing a fully-capped set of teeth, Hy Norman said, "As a matter of fact, I think we met during the 1972 McGovern campaign, of which, I am proud to say, I was a principal fundraiser."

Diana leaned across her desk to shake his hand. "No, I'm afraid not. Now, Hy, we're running a little late, so I'd like to get right to it. I have an idea for an hour television series and I'd like to lay it in your lap. Here's the back-up story. The hero is white-collar middle-class, an architect, aviation engineer, anything, a decent, law-abiding man. He lives with his wife and daughter in a large city. His wife and daughter are raped and he's mugged. He appeals to the police but their hands are tied by the Warren Court decisions. There's nothing but pornography in the movies, and vandals bomb his church. The animals are taking over. So he decides to take the law into his own hands. He buys a gun and practices till he's an expert. He takes up karate, becomes a black belt, adept in kung fu and all the other martial arts. He starts walking the streets of the city, decoying muggers into attacking him. He kung fus them all. Pretty soon, he's joined by a couple of neighbors. What we've got now is a vigilante group. That's the name of the show—'The Vigilantes.' The idea is, if the law won't protect the decent people, they have to take the law into their own hands."

"That's the most fascistic idea I've heard in years," Hy Norman said.

"Right."

"And a shameless steal from a movie called *Death Wish*."

"I know," Diana said. "And so far, *Death Wish* has grossed seventeen million, domestic. It obviously struck a responsive chord in Americans. I want to strike that same chord. Now, let me finish, Hy. The format is simple. Every week a crime is committed, and the police are helpless to deal with it. The victim turns to our group of vigilantes. What the hell, it's 'FBI,' 'Mission Impossible,' 'Kojak,' except the heroes are ordinary citizens, your neighbors and mine."

Hy Norman stood. "I find the whole thing repulsive."

"You give me a pilot script we can use as a 'Movie of the Week' for January, and I'll commit to twelve segments on the basis of that script."

Having started for the door, he turned back to face her.

"Come on, Hy," Diana said. "You've been knocking off these 'FBI'-'Mission Impossible'-type shows for years. Why do you think I'm laying this in your lap? You can bring me in a 'Movie of the Week' in January with your eyes closed."

"You'll commit to twelve segments on the basis of a pilot script?" he asked.

"That's what I said. Of course, we all know you're a highly principled liberal, and you may find this kind of show disgusting."

"Well, not necessarily," Hy Norman said, sitting down again. "I deplore vigilante tactics, of course, but the vigilante tradition is a profound, even a proud, tradition in the American social fabric. This sort of program also offers opportunities for coming to grips with the burning issues of our time, to do meaningful drama and at the same time providing mass entertainment."

"Beautiful, Hy," Diana said.

"Who do I talk numbers with, Charlie Kinkaid?"

"Right," Diana said. "I'll call Charlie and tell him we'll go to forty thousand for the first script. If you come up with anything good, Hy, I'll slot you on Wednesday nights at eight coming off 'The Howard Beale Show,' and that's the best lead-in you'll ever get."

Hy Norman opened the door to leave, looked out into the outer office, closed the door and turned to Diana.

"Is that Laureen Hobbs out there? What the hell is Laureen Hobbs doing out there?"

"We're going to put the Communist Party on prime-time television," Diana said.

"I wouldn't doubt it for a minute." He opened the door and left. On his heels, Glenn Kossoff ushered in Bill Herron; Laureen Hobbs, a handsome black woman of thirty-five in Afro and dashiki; Sam Haywood, in his late fifties, a shaggy, unkempt lawyer in the Clarence Darrow tradition, galluses, string-tie, folksy drawl and all; a young lawyer, Robert Murphy, early thirties, a Harvard intellectual type; and three agents from the William Morris office named Lennie, Wallie and Ed, all wearing trim blue suits and looking remarkably alike. Diana rose to greet them, extending her hand to Laureen Hobbs.

"Christ, you brought half the William Morris West Coast office with you. I'm Diana Christensen, a racist lackey of the imperialist ruling circles."

"I'm Laureen Hobbs," Laureen said, "a bad-ass Commie nigger."

"Sounds like the basis of a firm friendship," Diana said.

"This is my lawyer, Sam Haywood," Laureen said. All shook hands and sat down. A secretary moved around taking coffee orders.

"Well, Ms. Christensen," Sam Haywood said, "just what the hell's this all about? Because when a national television network in the person of bubby here," he indicated Herron, "comes to me and says he wants to put the ongoing struggle of the oppressed masses on prime-time television, I have to regard this askance."

Diana was about to answer, but he boomed along, beginning to hit his stride. "I have to figure this as an antithetical distraction. I don't suppose you're too well up on Marxist dialectic, but the thesis here, if you follow me, is that the capitalist state is in a terminal condition right now, and the antithesis is the maturation of the fascist state, of which you television people are correlative appendages. So when the correlative appendages of the fascist state come and say to me they want to give the revolution a weekly hour of prime-time television, I've got to figure this is a manifestation of a fascist antithesis. So you tell me—just what the hell is this all about?"

A hush followed Haywood's Hegelian instruction. Diana again tried to respond, but Haywood, in center-stage, was still in the full swell of rhetoric.

"Preventive co-optation, right? The ruling classes are running scared, right? You beat us bloody in our prisons. You turned the full force of your Cossack cops and paramilitary organs of repression against us. But you couldn't beat us down. Our numbers grew, our purpose swelled, and now the slave masters hear the rumble of revolution in their ears. So you have no alternative but to co-opt us. Put us on TV and pull our fangs. And we're supposed to sell out, right? For your gangster gold? Well, we're not going to sell out, baby! You can take your fascist TV and shove it right up your paramilitary ass! I'm here to tell you, we don't sell out! We don't want your gold! We're not going on TV!"

In the silence that followed, everybody digested this opening statement.

Diana sighed and muttered. "Oh, shit, Mr. Haywood, if you're not interested in my offer, why the hell did you bring two lawyers and three agents from the William Morris office?"

Murphy said coolly, "What Mr. Haywood was saying, Ms. Christensen, was that our client, Ms. Hobbs, wants it up front that the political content of the show has to be entirely in her control."

"She can have it," Diana said. "I don't give a damn about the political content."

"What kind of show'd you have in mind, Diana?" asked one of the agents.

"We're interested in doing a series based on the Ecumenical Liberation Army. But let's forget the idea of a weekly series for the moment and think of turning that bank ripoff footage into an hour-and-a-half 'Movie of the Week.' Let's say we open this movie with that bank ripoff footage and then we tell the story of how a rich young woman like Mary Ann Gifford becomes a flaming revolutionary. Would you people be interested in making such a movie for us? The political content of such a movie should suit you, since Mary Ann Gifford's conversion would involve a good deal of Marxist indoctrination."

"Not necessarily, Ms. Christensen," Laureen said. "The Ecumenical Liberation Army is an ultra-left sect creating political confusion with wildcat violence and pseudo-insurrectionary acts, which the Communist Party does not endorse. The American masses are not yet ready for open revolt. We would not want to produce a television show celebrating historically deviational terrorism."

"Even better," Diana said. "I see the story this way. Poor little rich girl is kidnapped by ultra-left sect. She falls in love with the leader of the gang, converts to his irresponsible violence. But then she meets you, understands the true nature of the ongoing people's struggle for a better society, and, in an emotion-drenched scene, she leaves her deviational lover and dedicates herself to you and the historical inevitability of the socialist state."

Laureen smiled. "That would be better, of course."

"I won't kid you, Ms. Hobbs," Diana said. "Your agitprop stuff will have to be crammed into two scenes. Mostly, this is a powerhouse love story of two typical young Americans caught in the vortex of contemporary chaos."

"Right on," Laureen said.

Diana turned to Lennie, Wallie and Ed. "Okay, you've got a go on the pilot script."

"What kind of numbers are we talking?" Ed asked.

"We'll give you our top deal, which I think is two-fifteen and twenty-five. You'll have to talk to Charlie Kinkaid about that. But as long as we're talking series, I'll tell you what I want. I want a lot more film like the bank ripoff the Ecumenicals sent in. The way I see this is, every week we open with the authentic footage of an act of political terrorism, taken on the spot and in the actual moment; then we go to the drama behind the opening film. Now I want you guys in series and on the air in September. That means I've got to have that pilot film in the can by the end of February at the outside. I want to put the pilot film on the air in March. If it's received well, we'll commit to fifteen with an option for ten more. The important thing is that authentic terrorist footage. That's what'll give us the shock and the power. That's your job, Ms. Hobbs. You've got to get the Ecumenicals to bring in that film for us. The network can't deal with them directly. They are, after all, wanted criminals."

"I don't like the glorification of ultra-left gangs," Laureen said.

"Ms. Hobbs," Diana said, "you are going to have to face some blunt facts about television. In television, you've got a show that goes on every week, so what's important is to set up a bunch of running characters that the audience will like and keep turning in every week to see. Okay, we've got this Ecumenical Liberation Army. To you, they're an ultra-left gang, and they may think of themselves as the heralds of a new world; but as far as I'm concerned, they're Robin Hood and his merry band of terrorists. I'm offering you an hour of prime-time television every week into which you can stick whatever propaganda you want. We're talking about thirty to fifty million people a shot. That's a lot better than handing out mimeographed leaflets on ghetto street corners."

"The Ecumenicals," Laureen said, "are an undisciplined gang, and the leader is an eccentric to say the least. He calls himself the Great Ahmed Khan and wears a hussar's shako."

"That's your headache. You're the *de facto* executive producer of this show and he's your star. All TV stars are nuts. If they aren't when they start, they sure get there by the end of the first season. But, if this show's a hit, and you can get three years out of it, you and the Communist Party will rake in millions. Which, I submit, is a hell of a lot more efficacious way of raising money than ripping off banks."

"I'll have to take this matter to the Central

Committee. And I'd better check this out with Ahmed Khan," Laureen said.

"I'll be in L.A. until Saturday and I'd like to get this thing rolling."

Laureen stood. "I'll get back to you as soon as I can."

Diana stood up as well. "I'm at the Beverly Hills Hotel."

By now they were all standing.

Lennie said, "Diana, you've got the guts of a linebacker."

"As racist lackeys of the imperialist ruling circles go," Laureen said, moving to the door, "you make one hell of a good one, Diana."

"And," Diana said, as she ushered them out, "you're one hell of a bad-ass Commie nigger."

"Sounds like the basis of a firm friendship," Laureen said, following the others out.

Diana closed the door, turned to Kossoff, Schlesinger and Herron and sighed.

"That's going to be our Wednesday night. Seven to eight, Howard Beale. Eight to nine, 'The Vigilantes.' Nine to ten, 'The Mao Tse-tung Hour.'"

"God, fascism and the revolution all on one night," Kossoff said.

"I guess that's what's called balanced programming," said Barbara Schlesinger.

"Okay," Diana said, rubbing her tired eyes, "who's next?"

Later in the Watts district of Los Angeles, Laureen Hobbs sat on the stoop of a peeling cottage talking to another member of the Central Committee, a middle-aged white man named

Witherspoon. The door opened behind them and a young white man in his twenties, wearing a fatigue jacket, torn Levis and dark sunglasses, poked his head out.

"Okay," he said.

Laureen and Witherspoon followed the man up the steps and into the entrance of the Ecumenicals' headquarters. Cartons, crates and newspapers were scattered about. A young black man stood on the stairway holding an army rifle. He followed Laureen and Witherspoon into the dining room.

Or what had been the dining room. Now, a naked overhead bulb was the only light. Sitting on a wooden folding chair was the Great Ahmed Khan, a powerful brooding black man in his early thirties. He wore a hussar's shako and the crescent moon on the Midianites hung from his neck. The chair he sat on was the only visible piece of furniture. There were two tattered sleeping bags on the floor, part of a general welter of old newspapers, empty grocery bags, fast-food hamburger wrappers. The walls were bare except for blowups of Che Guevara, Mao, Marlon Brando and Jane Fonda, scotch-taped to the peeling wallpaper. Automatic rifles leaned against the walls. Boxes of ammunition and grenades and mortar shells were stacked against a wall. Attending the Great Ahmed Khan were a young white man named Reynolds, a black woman in her late twenties named Jenkins, and a younger white woman, Mary Ann Gifford, who was a fire-eating militant with a bandolier of cartridges across her torn shirt and a submachine gun in her hands. Laureen pulled up an empty crate, sat, waved a limp hand of hello to the others and looked at the Great Khan.

"Well, Ahmed," she said, "you ain't going to believe this, but I'm going to make a TV star out of you. Just like Archie Bunker. You're going to be a household word."

"What the fuck are you talking about?" the Great Khan said.


Diana was in the shower. Barbara Schlesinger sat on the toilet with a couple of scripts in her lap, briefing her boss on the next day's activities.

"And then Goddard-Wilson Productions at three-thirty. That's a game show called 'Celebrity Checkers' that Lillian likes. They cover the whole studio floor with a giant black-and-white checkerboard. The checkers are chorus girls and chorus boys, and the two celebrities play checkers with these live checkers. The big thing is the smutty jokes that can be made, like 'you jump her,' and when the boys get to the other side they're called queens instead of kings, and the boys camp all over the place. . . ."

Diana stood with her eyes closed in the shower, just standing there, letting the water spray down on her. "Next," she said.

An hour or so later she sank onto the couch in her suite, staring blankly at the pile of scripts on the coffee table in front of her. She sighed a long shuddering, exhausted sigh, stood and went to the desk also piled high with scripts and contracts. Then she sat and picked up the phone.

"Room 237, please," she said. "Barbara, this is Diana. You know this town a lot better than I

do. Where do you go to get laid around here?"
She scribbled an address on a loose piece of
paper.

In a noisy, shrill gay bar, Diana moved through
the crush, scouting. She caught the eye of a stud
hustler, a male pin-up type with his shirt unbuttoned to the waist. He made his way to her.

"You go both ways?" Diana asked.

He nodded.

"How much?"

"Fifty bucks," he said.

"Let's go."

Some time later Diana lay on her bed staring
up at the ceiling as the stud serviced her. There
were tears streaming down her cheeks; it was
obviously an unhappy climax. She uttered a short
cry of consummation, sighed and closed her eyes.

"Okay, thanks," she said. "Your fifty bucks is
on the dresser. Beat it."

The stud got up and began dressing. The phone
rang. Diana didn't seem to hear it. It rang again.
Suddenly she began to cry, if it could be called
crying. The stud was at the bureau, fully dressed
now, counting his money. The phone rang again.
Diana shook her head and reached for it.

"Yes," she said. She could barely get the word
out.

Laureen Hobbs sat behind a desk at Communist Party Headquarters in Los Angeles talking on the telephone. In the background were
other members of the Central Committee, three
men, including Witherspoon, and two women.

"This is Laureen Hobbs, Ms. Christensen,"
Laureen said. "I'm sorry if I woke you, but you
said to call any time and I thought you'd like to

know we're ready to go ahead with that television series."

Sitting up, nude, alive again, Diana said, "Great! The William Morris Agency will package the show for you, get the writers and the actors and all that, but I'd appreciate your pushing them from your end because I want your pilot movie in the can by February and I want to put it on the air by March."

# CHAPTER 6

On Monday evening, January 27, 1975, a beaming announcer stepped to the microphone in the
news studio of the UBS building and called out,
"Ladies and gentlemen, let's hear it! How do you
feel?"

The audience roared back, *"We're mad as hell
and we're not going to take this any more!"*

"Ladies and gentlemen," the announcer
beamed, " 'The Network News Hour' . . ."

In the control room the monitor showed the
announcer's grinning face. "With Sybil the
Soothsayer, Jim Webbing and his It's-the-Emmes
Truth Department, Miss Mata Hari, tonight
another segment of Vox Populi and starring—"
There was a flourish of drums. "The mad prophet
of the airways, Howard Beale!"

A full symphony orchestra soared into an im-
perial crescendo and the houselights went to

black. The curtain rose slowly to reveal an absolutely bare stage except for one stained glass window suspended by wires high above the stage, through which shot an overpowering shaft of light as if emanating from heaven. Howard Beale, in an austere black suit with black tie, shambled on from the wings, found the spotlight and stood there for a moment, shielding his eyes from the blinding glare. The audience broke into tumultuous applause.

BEALE: Edward George Ruddy died today! Edward George Ruddy was the chairman of the board of the United Broadcasting Systems—the company that owns this network —and he died at eleven o'clock this morning of a heart condition. And woe is us, we're in a lot of trouble! So a rich little man with white hair died, what's that got to do with the price of rice, right? Why is that woe to us! Because you and sixty-two million other Americans are watching me right now, that's why! Because less than three percent of you people read books! Because less than fifteen percent of you read newspapers! Because the only truth you know is what you get over this tube! There is a whole and entire generation right now who never knew anything that didn't come out of this tube! This tube is the gospel! This tube is the ultimate revelation! This tube can make or break presidents, popes and prime ministers! This tube is the most awesome goddamned force in the whole godless world! And woe is us if it ever falls in the hands of the wrong people.

And that's why woe is us that Edward George Ruddy died. Because this network is now in the hands of CCA, the Communications Corporation of America. We've got a new chairman of the board, a man named Frank Hackett, now sitting in Mr. Ruddy's office on the twentieth floor. And when one of the largest companies in the world controls the most awesome goddamned propaganda force in the whole godless world, who knows what shit will be peddled for truth on this tube? So, listen to me! Television is not the truth! Television is a goddamned amusement park, that's what television is! Television is a circus, a carnival, a travelling troupe of acrobats and storytellers, singers and dancers, jugglers, sideshow freaks, lion-tamers and football players. We're in the boredom-killing business! If you want the truth, go to God, go to your guru, go to yourself—because that's the only place you'll ever find any real truth! But, man, you're never going to get any truth from us. We'll tell you anything you want to hear. We lie like hell! We'll tell you Kojak always gets the killer, and nobody gets cancer in Archie Bunker's house. And no matter how much trouble the hero is in, don't worry: just look at your watch—at the end of the hour, he's going to win. We'll tell you any shit you want to hear! We deal in illusion, man! None of it's true! But you people sit there—all of you—day after day, night after night, all ages, colors, creeds. We're all you know. You're beginning to believe this illusion we're spinning here.

You're beginning to think the tube is reality and your own lives are unreal. You do whatever the tube tells you. You dress like the tube, you eat like the tube, you raise your children like the tube, you think like the tube. This is mass madness, you maniacs! In God's name, you people are the real thing! We're the illusions! So turn off this goddamn set! Turn it off right now! Turn it off and leave it off. Turn it off right now, right in the middle of this very sentence I'm speaking now!

Sweating and red-eyed with his prophetic rage, Howard Beale collapsed to the floor in a prophetic swoon.

On that same day, Frank Hackett stood making his annual report in the conference room on the forty-third and forty-fourth floors of the CCA Building. It was a Valhalla of a room, dark and theatrical and enormous, with a shaft of light issuing from a slide projector onto a large screen on the raised podium. The screen showed charts of figures, one after the other, which accompanied Hackett's explication. Seated in a semicircular arrangement like a miniature United Nations were the 214 senior executives of the Communications Corporation of America. Each had his own desk with swivel chair, pinspot light, piles of bound company reports and nameplates with their names and companies they represented. One chair in the dead center of the first row swivelled back and forth, back and forth.

"UBS was running at a cash-flow break-even point," Hackett said, "after taking into account one hundred and ten million dollars of negative cash-flow from the network. Note, please, the added thirty-five million resulting from the issuance of the subordinated sinking debentures. It was clear the fat on the network had to be flitched off."

A new slide of charts flashed on the screen as the chair in the first row kept swivelling.

"Please note," Hackett continued, "comparative tables of first and third quarters, a diminution of more than five million in labor costs alone and a two million slash in capital expenditure programs. It is gratifying to report initial programming revenues in the projected amount of twenty-one million dollars, due to the phenomenal success of 'The Howard Beale Show.' I expect a positive cash-flow for the entire complex of forty-five million achievable in this fiscal year—a year, in short, ahead of schedule. I go beyond that. This network may well be the most significant profit center of the communications complex. And, based upon the rate of return on invested capital, the communications complex may well emerge as the towering and most profitable center in the entire CCA empire. I await your questions and comments. Mr. Jensen?"

The man who sat in the swivelling chair in the first row was Arthur Jensen, president and chairman of CCA, a short, balding, bespectacled man with a Grant Wood face.

"Very good, Frank," he said. "Exemplary. Keep it up."

Hackett basked in the praise.

On the following morning the body of Edward George Ruddy lay in state at Temple Emanu-El in New York. The vaulted reaches of the temple were packed with a standing-room audience of mourners. All the network brass were there.

Sitting in a pew, Max Schumacher's eyes met Diana Christensen's. She smiled, then looked back to the rabbi who was delivering the eulogy.

Outside, as a light snow fell, Max made his way through the crush to where Diana Christensen was standing with Nelson Chaney and Walter Amundsen.

Max said to Diana, "Buy you a cup of coffee?"

"Hell, yes."

They said goodbye to the others, then walked down Fifth Avenue. "Do you have to get back to the office?" Max asked.

"Nothing that can't wait."

They walked silently for a while.

"I drop down to the news studios every now and then and ask Howard Beale about you," Diana said. "He says you're doing fine. Are you?"

"No."

"Are you keeping busy?"

"After a fashion. This is the third funeral I've been to in two weeks. I have two other friends in the hospital whom I visit regularly. I've been to a couple of christenings. All my friends are dying or having grandchildren."

"You should be a grandfather about now. You have a pregnant daughter in Seattle, don't you?"

"Yes, my wife's out there now for the occasion. I've thought many times of calling you."

"I wish you had," Diana said.

They both suddenly stopped on Fifth Avenue between 65th and 64th streets to regard each other. Snowflakes moistened their cheeks, wetted their hair.

"I bumped into Sybil the Soothsayer in the elevator last week," Diana said. "I said: 'You know, Sybil, about four months ago you predicted I would get involved with a middle-aged man and so far, all that's happened is one many-splendored night. I don't call that getting involved.' And she said: 'Don't worry. You will.' It was a many-splendored night, wasn't it, Max?"

"Yes, it was."

"Are you going to get involved, Max?

"Yes, I need to get involved very much. How about you?"

"I've reached for the phone to call you a hundred times, but I was sure you hated me for taking your news show away."

"I probably did. I don't know any more. All I know is I can't keep you out of my mind."

They stared at each other, bemused by the abrupt explosion of their feelings. The snow drifted down. Pedestrians moved around them.

"My God, she's uncanny," Diana said.

"Who?"

"Sybil the Soothsayer. We've got a modern-day Greek drama here, Max. Two star-crossed lovers ordained by the gods to fall disastrously in love. A December-May story. Happily married middle-aged man meets desperately lonely young career woman, a violinist, let's say. They both know their illicit love can only end in tragedy, but they are cursed by the gods and plunge dementedly in love. For a few brief moments they are happy. He abandons devoted wife and loving children and she throws away her concert career.

Their friends plead with them to give each other up, but they are helpless playthings in the hands of malignant gods. Their love sours, embittered by ugly jealousies, sudden rancors. The soothsayer appears again and warns the girl she will die if she persists in this heedless love affair. She defies the soothsayer. But now one of the man's children is rushed to the hospital with a mysterious disease. He rushes back to his family, and she is left to throw herself on the railroad tracks. Give me a two-page outline on it, Max. I might be able to sell it to Xerox."

"A bit too austere for TV, I think."

"You're right. We couldn't get an eleven rating. How about a twist on *Brief Encounter*? Happily married man meets woman married to her career."

"NBC did *Brief Encounter* last year and it sank."

"Well," Diana said, "we're both a bit long in the tooth for *Romeo and Juliet*."

"Why don't we just wing it?"

She laughed. Then he laughed. A passerby glanced at them curiously.

# CHAPTER 7

Max and his wife were in the middle of an ugly scene. She sat erect on an overstuffed chair, her eyes wet with imminent tears. Max strode around the room, clearly under great stress.

"How long has it been going on?" she asked shrilly.

"A month. I thought at first it might be a transient thing and blow over in a week. I still hope to God it's just a menopausal infatuation. But it *is* an infatuation, Louise. There's no sense me saying I won't see her again, because I will. Do you want me to clear out, go to a hotel?"

"Do you love her?"

"I don't know how I feel. I'm grateful I still feel anything. I know I'm obsessed with her."

Louise rose to her feet. "Then say it! Don't keep telling me you're obsessed, you're infatuated —say you're in love with her!"

"I'm in love with her," Max said.

"Then get out, go to a hotel, go anywhere you want, go live with her! But don't come back! Because after twenty-five years of building a home and raising a family and all the senseless pain we've inflicted on each other, I'll be damned if I'll just stand here and let you tell me you love somebody else!" She strode around weeping, like a caged lioness.

"Because this isn't just some convention weekend with your secretary, is it? Or some broad you picked up after three belts of booze. This is your great winter romance, isn't it? Your last roar of passion before you sink into your emeritus years. Is that what's left for me? Is that my share? She gets the great winter passion and I get the dotage? Am I supposed to sit at home knitting and purling till you slink back like a penitent drunk? I'm your wife, damn it. If you can't work up a winter passion for me, then the least I require is respect and allegiance! I'm hurt! Don't you understand that?"

She stared at Max, her cheeks streaked with tears. After a moment he turned away from the glassed terrace doors and looked at his anguished wife.

"Say something, for God's sake!" she said.

"I've got nothing to say."

"Are you that deeply involved with her?"

"Yes."

"I won't give you up that easily, Max."

He embraced her, struggling to restrain his own tears. She released herself from his embrace.

"I think the best thing would be," Louise said, "if you move out. Does she love you, Max?"

"I'm not sure she's capable of any real feelings. She's the television generation. She learned life from Bugs Bunny. The only reality she knows is what comes over her TV set. She has devised a variety of scenarios for us all to play, as if it were a 'Movie of the Week.' And my God! Look at us, Louise. Here we are, going through the obligatory middle-of-Act-Two-scorned-wife-throws-peccant-husband-out scene. But no fear, I'll come back home in the end. All her plot outlines have me leaving her and returning to you because the audience won't buy a rejection of the happy American family. She does have one script in which I kill myself, an adapted-for-television version of *Anna Karenina* in which she's Count Vronsky and I'm Anna."

"You're in for some dreadful grief, Max."

"I know," he said.

On Friday morning, February 28, Diana murmured into her squawk box at the same time that she was putting things into a weekend bag. She was ebullient.

"I know what NBC offered them," she said. "Marty, so I'm saying, go to three point five, and I want an option for a third run on all of them. Marty, I'm in a big hurry and you and Charlie are supposed to be negotiating this, so goodbye and good luck and I'll see you Monday."

She clicked off her squawk box, snapped her weekend bag shut, whisked her sheepskin coat out of the closet and strode into her secretary's office. She found no one and continued out into the common room. Tommy Pellegrino saw her as he came out of his office.

"Jimmy Caan's agent just called and says absolutely nix," he said.

"You can't win them all," Diana said.

"Where can I reach you later today?"

"You can't. I'll be gone all weekend." She walked out.

Pellegrino turned to see Barbara Schlesinger coming out of her office. "I think the Dragon Lady got herself a dragon fellow."

"Poor bastard," Schlesinger said.

Diana, now wearing her coat and carrying her weekend bag, came striding happily out through the entrance door of the UBS building, heading for 55th Street. She spotted a double-parked car and headed through traffic to where Max waited in a rented Chevy. Leaning forward, he opened the door for her. She slipped into the front seat, nestled her head against his shoulder and they were off.

"NBC's offering three point two and a half mil per for a package of five James Bond pictures, and I think I'm going to steal them for three point five with a third run," she said happily. They moved out into heavy traffic on Sixth Avenue.

At dusk on a deserted beach in the Hamptons, the two lovers walked hand in hand. Diana was bubbling.

" 'The Vigilante Show,' " she said, "is sold firm. Ford took a complete position at, so help me, five-fifty CPM. In fact, I'm moving 'The Vigilante Show' to nine and I'm going to stick 'The Mao Tse-tung Hour' in at eight because we're having lots of trouble selling 'The Mao Tse-tung Hour.' This way we give it a terrific lead-in from 'The Howard Beale Show' and we'll back into the

Vigilantes, and it certainly ought to carry its own time slot. . . ."

Later at a small Italian restaurant, the obligatory romantic spot with checkered tablecloth, candles and wine, Diana and Max sat over dinner, utterly rapt.

Diana poured out her heart. "That 'Mao Tse-tung Hour' is turning into one big pain in the ass. We're having heavy legal problems with the federal government right now. Two FBI guys turned up in Hackett's office last week and served us with a subpoena. They heard about our San Mateo bank ripoff film, and they want it. We're getting around that by doing the show in collaboration with the News Division, so Hackett told the FBI to fuck off; we're standing on the First Amendment, freedom of the press, and the right to protect our sources. . . ."

Later still, they got out of their car in front of the motor court and headed for their ground-level room. While Max was unlocking the door, Diana kept talking. "Walter thinks we can knock out the misprision of felony charges . . ." They entered the room. Max flicked the light on, kicked the door shut and they were instantly in each other's arms in a passionate embrace.

"But he says absolutely nix on going to series," Diana continued. "They'll hit us with inducement and conspiracy to commit a crime." She removed her shoes, unbuttoned her blouse and whisked out of her slacks. In her bikini panties she groped along the walls of the darkened room, looking for a thermostat.

"Christ, it's cold in here," she said, turning up

the heat. "You see, we're paying these nuts from the Ecumenical Liberation Army ten thousand bucks a week to bring in authentic film footage on their revolutionary activities, and that constitutes inducement to commit a crime. Walter says we'll all wind up in federal prison."

Nearly naked, she entwined herself around Max, who had stripped to his trousers. The two hungry bodies slid down onto the bed.

Diana efficiently unbuckled and unzipped Max and continued her story, "I said: 'Walter, let the government sue us! We'll take them to the Supreme Court! We'll be front page for months! *The Washington Post* and *The New York Times* will be doing two editorials a week about us! We'll have more press than Watergate!' "

Groping, grasping, gasping and fondling they contrived to undress each other, and in a fever of sexual hunger, Diana mounted Max, voluptuously writhing and crying out. In the throes of passion, she said, "All I need—is six weeks of federal litigation—and 'The Mao Tse-tung Hour' —can start carrying its own time slot!" She screamed in consummation, sighed a long, deliciously shuddering sigh and sank softly into Max's embrace. For a moment, she rested her head on Max's chest, eyes closed in feline contentment.

After a moment, she purred. "What's really bugging me now is my daytime programming. NBC's got a lock on daytime with their lousy game shows, and I'd like to bust them. I'm thinking of doing a homosexual soap opera—'The Dykes'—the heartrending saga of a woman hopelessly in love with her husband's mistress. What do you think?"

Several days later, at the UBS building, Frank Hackett entered Screening Room Seven, joining Diana, Nelson Chaney, Walter Amundsen, Joe Donnelly and Arthur Zangwill. Diana buzzed the projectionist. "Okay," she said, "run it."

The room went dark. Hackett, sitting next to Diana, said, "I suppose Walter's told you he was in federal court yesterday about this thing, and so far, we're okay on the preliminary injunction but . . ."

The screen suddenly filled with black-and-white footage of a bank robbery. It was the same film that Diana had seen earlier but it was now spruced up, professionally edited and altogether presentable. The camera moved into the bank behind three men, two of them black, and two women, one black and one white. They dispersed to various parts of the bank. They were recognizable as members of the Ecumenical Liberation Army. The white man joined a short line, waited to be assigned to a teller's window; two others found places here and there where they could cover the various exists and doors. The black woman had a large tote bag slung over her shoulder. The white woman, Mary Ann Gifford, lugged a shopping bag. The film was silent, but over the footage, the voice of Mary Ann Gifford narrated:

GIFFORD: You are watching the ripoff of the Flagstaff National Bank which took place on Wednesday, September 18, 1974. This is not a reenactment. This is the actual robbery, filmed as it took place. . . .

Zangwill called to Diana, "Did you ever get those last releases?"

"We got them," she said.

GIFFORD: These are not actors; these are real people. . . .

The camera zoomed in on the Great Ahmed Khan, without his shako, at one of the desks, presumably writing out a series of deposit slips.

GIFFORD: This is Ahmed abd-Allah, the Great Khan of the Ecumenical Liberation Army . . .

The camera panned to pick up Dowling moving up in the waiting line.

GIFFORD: This is Fred Dowling . . .

Nelson Chaney asked, "How the hell did they shoot this film?"

"I'll be damned if I know," Diana said. "You ought to see the footage they have on the Folsom Prison riots."

The camera panned across the bank floor to Elwood Watkins who was asking a guard for a telephone directory.

GIFFORD: This is Elwood Watkins.

There was an abrupt cut to Mildred Jenkins rummaging through her tote bag for something.

GIFFORD: This is Mildred Jenkins.

There was a zoom to close-up, fuzzy at first and then focused on Mary Ann Gifford.

GIFFORD: And this is me. . . .

The camera pulled back to show Mary Ann bending over her shopping bag.

She whipped out a Czech service submachine gun 9 parabellum, pointed it to the ceiling and fired off a short warning burst, the sound of which erupted from the screen. There was an abrupt cut to ground-level, a wide angle shot, showing all the Ecumenicals with their weapons out and the Great Ahmed Khan shouting:

AHMED: This is a robbery! Everybody freeze!

There was a freeze frame on screen.
"We looped the voices," Diana said.

GIFFORD: I am Mary Ann Gifford, and this is my story . . .

On screen, the frame unfroze and the robbery could be seen in action. Hackett leaned over to Diana, "All right," he said, "we'll put the 'Mao Tse-tung' on in March. If it gets a decent rating we'll take a shot at a series with it."

A couple of weeks later, on Friday, March 14,

Max, looking domesticated in his shirt-sleeves and slippers, was taking two TV dinners from the stove in Diana's kitchen.

The story of Mary Ann Gifford, beautiful heiress turned revolutionary, was on the air. The day before, a federal grand jury, specifically convened for the purpose, handed down an indictment of the United Broadcasting Systems, charging misprision of felony, contempt of court, inducement to commit crime and criminal conspiracy.

Max moved out of the kitchen and headed for the living room as Diana entered. She was a little breathless, wearing a topcoat and extending a copy of the *New York Post*.

"Have you seen this yet?" she asked. "I tell you, if we paid the United States government to do this, they couldn't have timed it better."

Max looked at the front page of the *Post*. The lead story and banner headline took the right half of the page. But the left half of the front page was devoted to the grand jury's indictment. The headline read:

UBS FLAUNTS GOV'T INDICTMENT
WILL SHOW GIFFORD FILM.

"We're going to get a fifty share of this show, easy," Diana said, removing her coat and going into the living room where Max had already set up chairs and a table so they could watch TV and eat dinner at the same time. The TV console was on; the UBS hourly billboard and logo were on. Diana settled into her chair.

"I'm starving," she said.

The Mary Ann Gifford show began suddenly and silently on the console, the same footage that Diana had previously seen.

GIFFORD: You are watching the ripoff of the Flagstaff National Bank . . .

"A fifty share easy," Diana said, happily.

That March 14, when the Mary Ann Gifford show went on the air it got a 47 share in its first hour, climbing to a 51 during its second hour, showing sustained and increasing audience interest. The network promptly committed to fifteen shows with an option for ten more. There were, of course, the usual promotion difficulties.

At a small isolated farmhouse in Encino, a black limousine wound its way up the dirt road to the front porch. There the car was halted and checked out by an armed guard. Slivers of light crept out from behind the drawn shades of the farmhouse and angry voices could be heard. Two determined agents got out of the limousine—a young man, Freddie, carrying a large manila envelope, and a fat woman, Helen Miggs, who was carrying an attaché case. They went up the porch and into the house.

The farmhouse was the current headquarters of the Ecumenical Liberation Army and was no less a shambles than their previous one in Watts. The usual cartons, crates, newspapers, scraps of food, torn grocery bags, stacks of pamphlets, cases of weapons and ammunition, broken furniture and sleeping bags were everywhere. There seemed to be a conference going on in the living room. The two agents headed that way and saw Laureen Hobbs, the three William Morris agents, Wallie, Lennie and Ed, the Great Ahmed Khan, Mary Ann Gifford and other members of the group, wearing fatigues and bearing arms. There was also a middle-aged lawyer from International Creative Management named Willie Stein. All, with the exception of the Great Khan's retinue, were seated on broken chairs and cartons and crates and were studying eighty-page contracts, from which one of the agents was reading.

". . . herein called either 'the production fee' or 'overhead' equal to twenty percent, two-oh, except such percentage shall be thirty percent, three-oh, for ninety-minute or longer television programs," he mumbled.

Stein, a nervous man, addressed the newcomers, "Where the hell have you been?"

Helen Miggs embraced the Great Khan. "Ahmed, sweet," she said, "that dodo you sent for a driver couldn't find this fucking place."

There was a genial exchange of hellos and waves between the agents.

"Let's get on with this," Stein said, "before they raid this place, and we all wind up in the joint."

Ed, an agent, explained to Freddie, another agent, "We're on schedule A, page seven, small c, small i. . . ."

Helen whisked through her copy of the contract. "Have we settled that sub-licensing thing? We want a clear definition here. Gross proceeds should consist of all funds the sub-licensee receives, not merely the net amount remitted after payment to sub-licensee or distributor."

"We're not sitting still for overhead charges," Stein said, "as a cost prior to distribution."

Laureen, whose nerves had worn thin, exploded with rage: "Don't fuck with my distribution costs! I'm getting a lousy two-fifteen per segment, and I'm already deficiting twenty-five grand a week with Metro. I'm paying the agency ten percent off the top!" She pointed to the Great Khan, "And I'm giving this turkey ten thou a segment and another five for this fruitcake." She turned her head toward Mary Ann Gifford.

And Helen," Laureen went on, "don't start no shit with me about a piece again! I'm paying Metro twenty percent of all foreign and Canadian distribution, and that's after recoupment! The Communist Party's not going to see a nickel out of this goddamn show until we go into syndication!"

"Come on, Laureen," said Helen Miggs. "You've got the Party in there for seventy-five hundred a week in production expenses."

"I'm not giving this pseudo-insurrectionary sectarian a piece of my show!" Laureen was furious. "I'm not giving him script approval! And I sure as shit ain't cutting him in on my distribution charges!"

Mary Ann Gifford started screaming from the back. "Fuggin' fascist! Have you seen the movies we took at the San Marino jail break-out demonstrating the rising up of a seminal prisoner-class infrastructure!"

Laureen was not impressed. "You can blow the seminal prisoner-class infrastructure out of your ass! I'm not knocking down my goddamn distribution charges!"

The Great Khan offered his opinion by shooting his pistol off into the air. That gave everybody something to consider, especially Willie Stein, who was terrified.

"Man," the Great Khan said, "give her the fucking overhead clause."

"How did I get here?" Willie Stein said. "Who's going to believe this? I'm sitting here in a goddamn farm in Encino at ten o'clock at night negotiating overhead charges with cowboys!"

The Great Khan flipped through his copy of the contract. "Let's get to page twenty-two, five, small a, subsidiary rights . . ."

They all began flipping through their contracts.

"Where are we now?" Lennie asked.

"Page twenty-two," Wallie said, "middle of the page, subsidiary rights." He began to read, " 'As used herein, subsidiary rights means, without limitation, any and all rights with respect to theatrical motion picture rights, radio broadcasting, legitimate stage performances, printed publications (including but not limited to hardcover books, but excluding paperback books and comic books) and/or any other uses of a similar or dissimilar nature. . . .' "

At 6:30 P.M., Wednesday, May 28, in the grand ballroom of the Century Plaza Hotel in Los Angeles, about a thousand people in formal dress mingled for cocktails. Overhead, there was a huge banner reading UBS AFFILIATES 1975. The distinguished-looking crowd was slowly and noisily milling through the doors leading into the Grand Ballroom.

There were Herb Thackeray, Norman Moldanian and their wives, the general manager of WJGL, Cincinnati, and his wife, the general manager of KBEX, Albuquerque, and his wife, as well as the sales manager of that station and his wife. There was chatter and small talk, laughter and general good cheer. Frank Hackett and his wife were talking with some other general managers and program directors and sales managers of various affiliates and their wives.

Diana, radiantly beautiful in an evening gown, leaned down from the dais to accept congratulations from well-wishers.

"Millard Villanova, sales manager, KGIM, Boise. My wife, here, Maureen . . ."

"My pleasure," Diana said.

"I just want to tell you," he said, "we saw your great stuff this afternoon, Di. It was great."

"Great, Millard," Diana said. She turned to accept other enthusiastic greetings from another general manager and his wife being brought down the dais to her by Walter Amundsen.

A little later, everybody was seated at tables, listening to an address by Nelson Chaney, president of the UBS network, who was spotlighted at the podium.

"Over the past two days," he said, "you've all had an opportunity to meet Diana Christensen, our vice-president in charge of programming. This afternoon, you all saw some of the stuff she's set up for the new season. You all know she's the woman behind 'The Howard Beale Show.' We know she's beautiful. We know she's brainy. I just think, before we start digging into our Chateaubriands, we ought to let her know how we feel about her."

There was an ovation from the audience. In response to Chaney's beckoning, Diana rose from her chair in the shadow of the dais and came down to the podium. She stood there, showered with applause, beaming, exultant.

"We've got the number one show in television!" Diana said. Applause. "And, at next year's affiliates' meeting, I'll be standing here telling you we've got the top five!" There was tumult.

While Diana spoke, an assistant manager leaned over to Frank Hackett and murmured to him.

"Last year," Diana continued, "we were the number four network. Next year, we're number one!" More tumult.

Frank Hackett rose, murmured apologies to his neighbors and followed the assistant manager out of the ballroom.

"It is exactly seven o'clock here in Los Angeles," Diana said. "And right now over a million homes using television in this city are turning their dials to Channel 3—and that's our channel."

In the cocktail area of the Grand Ballroom a portable TV set perched on the bar. There was music, a rolling of kettledrums and a trumpet fanfare. The announcer was saying, "Ladies and gentlemen! Let's hear it! How do you feel?"

And the TV studio audience roared happily, *"We're mad as hell and we're not going to take this any more!"*

The cocktail area was being cleared away by a staff of waiters and busboys—hors d'oeuvres and liquor were being removed, tables and chairs were being packed up. A couple of waiters were watching 'The Howard Beale Show' on the portable TV set.

> STUDIO ANNOUNCER: Ladies and gentlemen—the mad prophet of the airways—*Howard Beale!*

On the TV set the houselights went down, the curtain rose and, as before, there was a bare stage, a shimmering stained glass window, an ethereal shaft of light, and Howard Beale in his austere black suit trudged out and exploded:

> BEALE: All right, listen to me! Listen carefully! This is your goddamn life I'm talking about today! In this country, when one company takes over another company, they simply buy up a controlling share of the stock. But first they have to file notice with the government and with the stockholders of the company they're buying up. That's how CCA—the Communications Corporation of America—bought up the company that owns this network. And now somebody's buying up CCA! Some company named Western World Funding Corporation is buying up CCA! They filed their notice this morning! Well, just who the hell is Western World Funding Corporation? It's a consortium of banks and insurance companies who are not buying CCA for themselves but as agents for somebody else!

Frank Hackett walked into the cocktail area and waited while his assistant got a waiter to bring a telephone to one of the tables still standing.

BEALE: Well, who's this somebody else? They won't tell you! They won't tell you, they won't tell the Senate, they won't tell the SEC, the FCC, the Justice Department, they won't tell anybody! They say it's none of our business! The hell it ain't!

Hackett spoke into his telephone. "This is Mr. Hackett, do you have a call for me?" He called to the cluster of waiters around the TV set, "Do you want to turn that down, please?"

BEALE: Well I'll tell you who they're buying CCA for. They're buying it for the Saudi Arabian Investment Corporation! They're buying it for the Arabs!

Hackett was the hearty executive on the phone. "Clarence? Frank Hackett here! How's everything back in New York? How's the good lady?" His face sobered. "All right, take it easy, Clarence. I don't know what you're talking about. . . . When? Clarence, take it easy. 'The Howard Beale Show' is just going on out here. You guys get it three hours earlier in New York. Clarence, take it easy. How the hell could I see it? It's just on now. Well, when did Mr. Jensen call you?"

BEALE: We know the Arabs control more than sixteen billion dollars in this country! They own a chunk of Fifth Avenue, twenty downtown pieces of Boston, a part of the port of New Orleans, an industrial park in Salt Lake City. They own big hunks of the Atlanta Hilton, the Arizona Land and Cattle Company, the Security National Bank in California, the Bank of the Commonwealth in Detroit! They control ARAMCO, so that puts them into Exxon, Texaco and Mobil Oil! They're all over—New Jersey, Louisville, St. Louis, Missouri! And that's only what we know about! There's a hell of a lot more we don't know about because all those Arab petrodollars are washed through Switzerland and Canada and the biggest banks in this country!

Hackett peered over the shoulder of a waiter to watch the TV screen.

BEALE: What we don't know is this CCA deal and all the other CCA deals!

Hackett winced.

BEALE: Right now, the Arabs have screwed us out of enough American dollars to come back and, with our own money, buy General Motors, IBM, ITT, AT&T, DuPont, U.S. Steel and twenty other top American companies, and there's no way of knowing they haven't already done that.

Hackett, Nelson Chaney, Walter Amundsen and Diana Christensen, still wearing their dinner clothes, sat in a dark, smallish videotape room cluttered with electronic equipment watching a replay of "The Howard Beale Show" on a big screen. Two technicians fiddled with the equipment.

BEALE: Now, listen to me, goddamnit! The Arabs are simply buying us! They're buying all our land, our whole economy, the press, the factories, financial institutions, the government! They're going to own us! A handful of agas, shahs and emirs who despise this country and everything it stands for—democracy, freedom, the right for me to get up on television and tell you about it—a couple of dozen medieval fanatics are going to own where you work, where you live, what you read, what you see, your cars, your bowling alleys, your mortgages, your schools, your churches, your kids, your whole life!

Amundsen muttered, "The son of a bitch is effective, all right."

BEALE: And there's not a single law on the books to stop them! There's only one thing that can stop them—you! So I want you to get up now. I want you to get out of your chairs and go to the phone. Right now. I want you to go to your phone or get in your car and drive into the Western Union office in town. I want everybody listening to me to get up right now and send a telegram to the White House!

Hackett sighed in anguish, "Oh, God!"

BEALE: By midnight tonight I want a million telegrams in the White House! I want them wading knee-deep in telegrams at the White House! Get up! Right now! And send the president a telegram saying: 'I'm mad as hell and I'm not going to take this any more! I don't want the banks selling my country to the Arabs! I want this CCA deal stopped!'

"Oh, God!" Hackett said again.

BEALE: I want this CCA deal stopped now! I want this CCA deal stopped now!

Suddenly, Howard Beale collapsed in his now familiar prophetic swoon. On screen, attendants came and carried him off.

Chaney spoke to a technician. "Is that it, does he come back later in the show?"

"That's it. This is one of those shows he just zonks out."

"Do you want to see any more?" Chaney asked Hackett who sat in numb silence. "All right, turn it off," Chaney said.

"Do you want to go to your office?" Amundsen asked Hackett, who stared silently into space.

"Look," Chaney said to the technicians, "could we have the room?"

"Sure." They left.

In the silence that followed, Amundsen stretched and rose to his feet. "Well," he said, I'd like to see a typescript and run it a couple of times, but as for this whole CCA deal with the Saudis, you'd know a lot more about that than I would, Frank. Is it true?"

Hackett sighed and mumbled. "Yes. CCA has two billion in loans with the Saudis, and they hold every pledge we've got. We need that Saudi money bad." He stood, so wretched he was tranquil. "A disaster. This show is a disaster, an unmitigated disaster, the death knell. I'm ruined, I'm dead, I'm finished."

"Maybe we're overstating Beale's clout with the public."

"An hour ago," Hackett said, "Clarence McElheny called me from New York. It was ten o'clock in the East, and our people in the White House report they were already knee-deep in telegrams. By tomorrow morning, they'll be suffocating in telegrams."

"Well," Chaney asked, "can the government stop the deal?"

"They can hold it up. The SEC could hold this deal up for twenty years if they wanted to. I'm finished. Any second that phone's going to ring and Clarence McElheny is going to tell me Mr. Jensen wants me in his office tomorrow morning so he can personally chop my head off. I would like to be alone now so I can make my peace with God." Tears were streaming down his cheeks as he shuffled, a broken man, around the room. "Four hours ago, I was the Sun God at CCA, Mr. Jensen's handpicked golden boy, the heir apparent. CCA was my whole life! CCA was my home, God and country! Now I'm a man without a corporation!"

Diana came off the back wall. "Let's go back

to Howard Beale. You're not seriously going to pull Beale off the air?"

"Mr. Jensen is unhappy with Howard Beale," Hackett said, "and wants him discontinued."

"He may be unhappy, but he isn't stupid enough to withdraw the number one show on television out of pique."

Hackett exploded. "Two billion dollars isn't pique! That's the wrath of God! And the wrath of God wants Howard Beale fired!"

"What for? Every other network will grab him the minute he walks out the door. He'll be back on the air tomorrow. We'll have to pay off his contract. It's going to cost you five million bucks just to keep him off the air."

"Then it'll cost five million bucks!" Hackett screamed.

"And we'll lose twenty points in audience share in the first week," Diana said, "roughly forty million loss in revenues for the year. That has to give even Arthur Jensen pause. And on top of that, Beale could sue the shit out of us."

"I'm going to kill Howard Beale!" Hackett said. "I'm going to impale the son of a bitch with a sharp stick through the heart!"

"And let's not discount federal action by the Justice Department. If CCA pulls Beale off the air as an act of retribution, that's a flagrant violation of network autonomy and an egregious breach of the articles of acquisition."

Hackett was beginning to like his new train of thought. "I'll take out a contract on him. I'll hire professional killers. I'll do it myself. I'll strangle him with a sashcord."

"If we pull Beale off the air," Diana persisted,

"the public outcry will be twice what it is today. No, I don't think Jensen will fire Howard Beale."

"Somebody's got to be fired!" Hackett said. "You don't blow two billion dollars without somebody being fired!"

"Are you figuring on me for this ritual sacrifice?"

Hackett contemplated Diana with a steely look, once more in control of himself. "Right now, you're not expendable."

"Jensen isn't going to fire anybody," Diana said. "He's sitting up there in his office surrounded by lawyers and senior vice-presidents, and right about now, they've begun to realize the extraordinary impact of television. That impact can be focused, manipulated, utilized. If Howard Beale can hurt them, he can help them."

The telephone rang. After a moment of anxious silence, Hackett picked it up.

"Yes, Clarence, I've already booked my flight. . . . Well, can you give me a little more time than that? I've got the red-eye flight and I won't be back in New York until six tomorrow morning. That'll be just fine. I'll see you then." He returned the phone to its cradle and regarded Diana for a moment.

"Mr. Jensen wants to meet Howard Beale personally. He wants Mr. Beale in his office at ten o'clock tomorrow morning."

# CHAPTER 8

Next morning a black limousine pulled up in front of the CCA building in New York City. Frank Hackett and Howard Beale, both dressed in banker's gray, got out of the car and moved to the building entrance. Hackett herded Beale along. Howard was clearly in a beatific state, his eyes glistening transcendentally, smiling the smile of the elevated spirit.

Hackett clutched Beale's elbow and tried to move him along to the tower elevators in the back of the lobby, but Howard suddenly pulled up abruptly, raised his arms over his head and announced at the top of his lungs:

"The final revelation is at hand! I have seen the shattering fulgurations of ultimate clarity! The light is impending! I bear witness to the light!"

This outburst didn't seem to bother most of

the people in the lobby, except for one or two who murmured, "Hey, that's Howard Beale, isn't it?" The outburst did appall Frank Hackett, who looked distressed as he clutched at Howard's arm to get him moving again.

Arthur Jensen's office was enormous, two walls of windows towering over the Manhattan landscape, through which the sunlight streamed in. Jensen rose from behind his massive desk.

"Good afternoon, Mr. Beale," Jensen said. "They tell me you're a madman."

"Only desultorily," Beale said, closing the door behind himself.

"How are you now?" Jensen asked.

Howard, who seemed as mad as a hatter, said, "I'm mad as a hatter."

"Who isn't? Don't sit down. I'm taking you to our conference room, which seems more seemly a setting for what I have to say to you."

He took Howard's arm and moved him to a large oaken door leading out of Jensen's office.

"I started as a salesman, Mr. Beale," Jensen continued. "I sold sewing machines and automobile parts, hair brushes and electronic equipment. They say I can sell anything. I'd like to try and sell something to you."

They passed into the conference room in the CCA building. It was the same overwhelming cathedral of a conference room where Frank Hackett had given his annual report. He had spoken in darkness. Now the enormous curtains were up and an almost celestial light poured in through the huge windows. Being on the forty-third and forty-fourth floors, the sky outside was only sporadically interrupted by the towers of other skyscrapers. The double semi-circular bank of seats was empty. The effect was one of hushed vastness.

"Valhalla, Mr. Beale," Jensen said. "Please sit down."

He led Howard down the steps to floor level while he, himself, ascended to the small stage and then to the podium. Howard sat in one of the two hundred-odd seats. Jensen pushed a button and the enormous drapes slowly fell, slicing away layers of light until the vast room was utterly dark. Then, the little pinspots on each of the desks popped on, including the one in front of Howard, creating a miniature Milky Way. A shaft of white light shot out from the rear of the room and fastened on Jensen on the podium, a sun in his own galaxy. Behind him was the shadowed white of the lecture screen. Jensen suddenly wheeled on his audience of one and roared out:

"You have meddled with the primal forces of nature, Mr. Beale, and I won't have it, is that clear? You think you have merely stopped a business deal—that is not the case! The Arabs have taken billions of dollars out of this country, and now they must put it back. It is ebb and flow, tidal gravity, it is ecological balance! You are an old man who thinks in terms of nations and peoples. There are no nations! There are no peoples! There are no Russians. There are no Arabs! There are no third worlds! There is no West! There is only one holistic system of systems, one vast and immane, interwoven, interacting, multi-variate, multinational dominion of dollars! Petrodollars, electrodollars, multidollars, reichsmarks, rubles, rin, pounds and shekels! It is the international system of currency that determines the totality of life on this planet! That is the natural order of things today! That is the atomic, subatomic and galactic structure of things today! And you have meddled with the primal forces of nature and you will atone! Am I getting through to you, Mr. Beale?"

In the darkness, Howard said, "Amen."

"You get up on your little twenty-one inch screen, Mr. Beale," Jensen resumed, "and howl about America and democracy. There is no America. There is no democracy. There is only IBM and ITT and AT&T and Du Pont, Dow, Union Carbide and Exxon. Those are the nations of the world now. What do you think the Russians talk about in their councils of state—Karl Marx? They pull out their linear programming charts, statistical decision theories and minimax solutions like the good little systems-analysts they are and compute the price-cost probabilities of their transactions and investments just like we do.

"We no longer live in a world of nations and ideologies, Mr. Beale. The world is a college of corporations, inexorably determined by the immutable bylaws of business. The world is a business, Mr. Beale! It has been that way since man crawled out of the slime, and our children, Mr. Beale, will live to see that perfect world without war and famine, oppression and brutality—one vast and ecumenical holding company, for whom all men will work to serve a common profit, in which all men will hold a share of stock, all necessities provided, all anxieties tranquillized, all boredom amused. And I have chosen you to preach this evangel, Mr. Beale."

"Why me?" Howard whispered humbly.

"Because you're on television, dummy. Sixty million people watch you every night of the week, Monday through Friday."

Howard slowly rose from the blackness of his seat so that he was lit only by the ethereal diffusion of light shooting out of the rear of the room. He stared at Jensen, spotted on the podium, transfixed.

"I have seen the face of God!" Howard said.

Jensen considered this curious statement for a moment. "You just might be right, Mr. Beale."


That evening, Howard Beale went on the air to preach the corporate cosmology of Arthur Jensen. He seemed sad, resigned, weary.

BEALE: Last night, I got up here and asked you people to stand up and fight for your heritage and you did and it was beautiful. Six million telegrams were received at the White House. The Arab takeover of CCA has been stopped. The people spoke, the people won. It was a radiant eruption of democracy. But I think that was it, fellers. That sort of thing isn't likely to happen again. Because in the bottom of all our terrified souls, we all know that democracy is a dying giant, a sick, sick, dying, decaying political concept, writhing in its final pain. I don't mean the United States is finished as a world power. The United States is the most powerful, the richest, the most advanced country in the world, light-years ahead of any other country. And I don't mean the Communists are going to take over the world. The Communists are deader than we are. What's finished is the idea that this great country is dedicated to the freedom and flourishing of every individual in it. It's the individual that's finished. It's the single, solitary human being who's finished. Because this is no longer a nation of independent individuals. This is a nation of two hundred-odd million, transistorized, deodorized, whiter-than-white, steel-belted bodies, totally unnecessary as human beings and as replaceable as piston rods. . . .

It was a perfectly admissible argument that Howard Beale advanced in the days that followed; it was, however, also a very tedious one. By the end of the first week in June 'The Howard Beale Show' had dropped one point in the ratings, and its trend of shares dipped under 48 for the first time since November. Hysteria swept through the network.

Diana Christensen pushed through the glass doors of her department offices, called to George Basch as she strode to her office, barked something at her secretary and plunked herself down behind her desk. A moment later George Basch entered.

"I don't know," Diana said to him. "How long is Beale going to go on with that corporate shit? I just left the son of a bitch: he's impenetrable.

So I think we better start shoring up the dikes and plugging the floodgates."

Barbara Schlesinger entered. Diana paused and then resumed. "Just to play safe, let's start scouting around for possible replacements. I hear ABC's grooming a mad prophet of their own in Chicago as our competition for next season. See if you can get a tape on him, Barbara. Maybe we can steal him. Also start getting some tapes on hot young anchormen around the country. And let's start building up the other segments of the show: Sybil the Soothsayer, Jim Webbing. The Vox Populi segment is catching on; let's make that a daily feature. Just in case we have to lose Howard, I want the rest of the show to be as strong as possible."

That night on the network news show, Howard Beale again spoke on the screen.

BEALE: What I'm talking about, of course, is dehumanization. That's a bad word, dehumanization, like imperialism, military-industrial complex, big-business. We're all supposed to resist dehumanization. Lord knows, I've been getting up on this program for eight months and that's all I've been yelling about —we must fight the dehumanization of the spirit. I kept yelling all the good words like justice and brotherhood, the dignity of man, compassion, decency and simple human kindness. Well, we all know that's a lot of shit. I mean, just look around you. So the time has come to say: is dehumanization such a bad word? Because good or bad, that's what is so. And we are moving inexorably

towards more total dehumanization, drawn
by gravitational forces far greater than anything we can comprehend. And not just us,
the whole world.

We're just the most advanced country, so
we're getting there first. The rest of the world
—Russia, China, the undeveloped world—
can't wait to catch up to us. It'll be easy for
them. They're already dedicated to mass so-
cieties. The whole world then is becoming
humanoid, creatures that look human but
aren't. We are becoming mass-produced,
programmed, wired—insensate things useful only to produce and consume other mass-
produced things, all of them as unnecessary
and useless as we are. Nevertheless, that is
the cosmic state of affairs.

Once you've grasped that, once you've
understood the total futility and purposeless-
ness of human existence, then the whole
universe becomes orderly and comprehen-
sible. We are no longer an industrialized
society; we aren't even a post-industrial or
technological society. We are now a corporate
society, a corporate world, a corporate universe. This world is a vast cosmology of
small corporations orbiting around larger
corporations who, in turn, revolve around
giant corporations, and this whole endless,
eternal, ultimate cosmology is expressly designed for the production and consumption
of useless things. . . .

By the end of June, "The Howard Beale Show"
was down eleven points, a catastrophic con-

dition. In six weeks, Howard Beale who had been a national glory had become an outbreak of plague.

On Tuesday, July 1, at 3:00 P.M., Diana Christensen, followed by Joe Donnelly, strode into the busy nightly news room. They entered Howard Beale's office, interrupting an urgent colloquy between Howard and his agent, an ordinarily urbane gentleman named Lew Weiskopf—who, at the moment, was clearly agitated.

Diana spoke without preamble. "You are small-pox, Howard! You are *typhoid*." She dropped a booklet she was carrying onto his desk. "In case you haven't seen this week's rating book, your share was thirty-eight last week! You killed another three million listeners! You're going to wipe out the whole population if you keep this up! You are driving me nuts, Howard!" Then she turned to make introductions.

"Lew Weiskopf, Joe Donnelly, our VP sales. Lew is Howard's agent. Close the door, Harry," she said, as Harry Hunter came in.

"I asked Lew to be here," Diana said, "because I don't want anybody saying later I didn't make myself clear. I'm sick of arguing with your client, Lew. I've brought Joe Donnelly down here to personally tell you the advertisers have started to call him directly."

"McCann-Erickson told me flatly," Donnelly said, "they're bailing out."

"I can say only what my voices tell me to say," Howard said.

"Well, fire them!" Diana said. "We'll get you new voices. We'll call the Writers Guild and get you all the goddamn voices you want! Lew here represents a thousand voices. We'll get you the best voices in the business! We want you to go back to being crazy!"

Howard, rising to his feet, cried out, "I'm not an actor! I can't get up and perform mad scenes for you! I am impelled by an inner force! I do what I am told to do! I say what I am told to say! I have no control over it."

A sad silence greeted this outburst. Diana sank wearily into a chair and sighed. The others stared helplessly at the floor.

After a moment, Diana said, "Howard, I am taking you off the air. As of tonight, you're on vacation."

"As of tonight?" Harry Hunter exclaimed.

"As of tonight. I've got fifty other hours of programming to worry about. I'll level with you, Lew. We're looking around for replacements. I'm going up to look at audition tapes right now. The network has to protect itself."

In the ninth floor screening room, an imposing Mosaic figure glowed on a large screen. He was fully bearded and wore ankle-length black robes, thonged sandals and was standing on a lonely mountain spur, inveighing against the idolatries of the world. The screening room was half-filled with network and programming executives— Diana, Barbara, Tommy Pellegrino, Frank Hackett, Nelson Chaney, Herb Thackeray, Joe Donnelly and Harry Hunter. From the screen, the Mosaic figure ranted.

Diana suddenly stood in the shaft of light coming from the projector. "No, damn it!" she said. "If we wanted hellfire we'd get Billy Graham! We don't want faith-healers, tent-show evangelists, or Oberammergau passion-players. What about that terrific new messiah ABC was supposed to have signed up as our competition?"

"That's him," Pellegrino said, indicating the screen.

"That's him?" Diana said.

"Yeah."

"Jesus, turn him off."

The screen went blank.

"How about that guy who's supposed to be killing them in some local station in California?" Thackeray said.

"I saw him," said Schlesinger. "Straight out of Cecil B. De Mille."

Diana asked Pellegrino, "How many more have you got?"

"I've got three more," Pellegrino said, "but you've already seen the best ones. I've got a guru from Spokane and two more hellfires who see visions of the Virgin Mary."

Diana sank into her chair and turned to Hackett in the row immediately behind her.

"We're not going to find a replacement for Howard Beale," she said. "So let's stop kidding ourselves. Full-fledged messiahs don't come in bunches. We either go with Howard or we go without him. My reports say we'll do better without him. It would be disaster to let this situation go on even another week. By then, he'll be down another sixteen points and the trend will be irreversible. I think we should fire Howard."

"Arthur Jensen," Hackett said, "has taken a strong personal interest in 'The Howard Beale Show.' "

"I know," Diana said, "and I know you're

having dinner with Jensen tonight. I think you should put it to him straight. Howard Beale is a repellent. He turns people off. He's hurting the shows that precede him and threatening the ones that follow him. We'll have to fire him."

Hackett sighed gloomily and addressed the room at large. "We'll have to do something. Let me talk to Jensen and then let's meet in my office at ten o'clock tonight. Diana, give me copies of all your audience research reports. I may need them for Jensen. Is ten o'clock convenient for everyone?"

Apparently it was.

At eight o'clock that evening, Diana let herself into her apartment. The foyer was dark and she moved to the living room. There, Max had fallen asleep on one of the soft chairs, a newspaper in his lap. His mouth was agape and he wheezed. In the stark lighting of the lamp behind the chair, Diana stood, regarding him with perceptible distaste. She slipped out of her jacket and went into the bedroom.

Later, in her brightly lighted bedroom, Diana, freshly scrubbed and in a robe, was packing Max's things. A large valise lay open on the bed and Diana was fetching Max's suits from the closet, folding them and packing them away. Max appeared rumpled and in his shirtsleeves in the doorway behind her. She sensed his presence, gave him a glance, and continued with her packing.

"I think the time has come," she said, "to re-evaluate our friendship."

"So I see," Max said.

"I don't like the way this script of ours is turning out. The whole thing started as a comedy, remember? Now it's turning into a seedy little drama. Middle-aged man leaves wife and family for young, heartless woman, goes to pot. *The Blue Angel* with Marlene Dietrich and Emil Jannings. I don't like it."

"So you've decided to cancel the show."

"Right."

"Listen, I'll do that," Max said, moving over to the bed to do the packing. She sat on one of the chairs.

"I know your daughter got in from Seattle this morning," Diana said, "and you had lunch with her and your new grandson. I'm sure it was a difficult meeting. I know how deeply upset you are by the pain you've caused your family. The simple fact is you're a family man, Max. You like a home and kids, and that's beautiful. But I'm incapable of any such commitment. All you'll get from me is another couple of months of intermittent sex and ugly little scenes like the one we had last night. I'm sorry for all those vicious things I said to you. You're not the worst fuck I've ever had. Believe me, I've had worse. And you don't puff and snorkle and make death-rattles. As a matter of fact, you're rather serene in the sack."

Max had gone into the bathroom for his toilet articles and when he came out, he regarded Diana for a moment.

"Why do women always think the most savage thing they can do to a man is to impugn his cocksmanship?"

"I'm sorry I impugned your cocksmanship."

"I stopped comparing genitals back in the schoolyard," Max said.

"You're being docile as hell about this."

"Hell, Diana," he said, "I knew it was over between us weeks ago."

"Will you go back to your wife?"

"I'll try, but I don't think she'll jump at it. But don't worry about me. I'll manage. I always have, I always will. I'm more concerned about you. Once I go, you'll be back in the grip of your own desolate terrors. Fifty dollar studs and the nightly sleepless contemplation of suicide. You're not the boozer type, so I figure a year, maybe two, before you crack up or jump out your fourteenth floor office window."

Diana stood. "Stop selling, Max," she said. "I don't need you." She left the room and went into the kitchen, where a kettle was steaming. She fetched a cup and saucer and was about to make some instant coffee when she was overtaken by a curious spasm. Her hand holding the cup and saucer shook so much she had to put them down. With visible effort, she pulled herself together and went into the living room. There she stood, shouting to Max through the bedroom doorway.

"I don't want your pain! I don't want your menopausal decay and death! I don't need you, Max!"

"You need me badly! I'm your last contact with human reality! I love you, and that painful, decaying menopausal love is the only thing between you and the shrieking nothingness you live the rest of the day!" He slammed the valise shut.

"Then don't leave me!"

"It's too late, Diana! There's nothing left in you that I can live with! You're one of Howard's humanoids, and if I stay with you, I'll be destroyed. Like Howard Beale was destroyed. Like everything you and the whole institution of television touch gets destroyed! You are indifferent to all suffering, insensitive to joy. All of life is reduced to the common rubble of banality. War, murder, death are all the same to you as bottles of beer. The daily business of life is a corrupt comedy. You even shatter sensations into jagged fragments of minutes, split-seconds and instant replays. You are madness incarnate, Diana, virulent madness, and whatever you touch dies with you. Well, not me! Not while I can still feel pleasure and pain and love! Oh, shit, Diana, it's over with us. I'm not sure it ever really happened, but I know it's over."

He turned back to his valise and buckled it. Diana sank into a chair. A moment later, Max came out of the bedroom, lugging a raincoat as well as the valise. He lugged his way across the living room, then paused for a moment, reflecting.

"It's a happy ending, Diana. Wayward husband comes to his senses, returns to his wife with whom he has built a long and sustaining love. Heartless young woman is left alone in her arctic desolation. Music up with a swell. Final commercial. And here are a few scenes from next week's show."

He disappeared down the foyer. Diana could hear the front door being opened and closed. She sat in her chair, pulling her robe around her, alone.

At 10:15 P.M. Frank Hackett walked down the long, empty, hushed corridor to the large double doors of his office—it had originally belonged to Edward Ruddy. Nelson Chaney was waiting for him there.

"How'd it go?" Chaney asked.

Hackett sighed.

Thackeray and Donnelly and Diana Christensen were waiting in the outer foyer and all followed into Hackett's office. The nighttime grandeur of Manhattan glimmered below them. As all the others found places around the room, Hackett spoke.

"Mr. Jensen was unhappy because Howard Beale was not on the air tonight. Mr. Jensen thinks Howard Beale is bringing a very important message to the American people, so he wants Howard Beale on the air tomorrow. And he wants him kept on." He looked around the room but nobody had anything to say.

Hackett continued. "Mr. Jensen feels we are being too catastrophic in our thinking. I argued that television was a volatile industry in which success and failure were determined week by week. Mr. Jensen said he did not like volatile industries and suggested with a certain sinister silkiness that volatility in business usually reflected bad management. He didn't really care if Howard Beale was the number one show in television or the fiftieth. He didn't really care if 'The Howard Beale Show' lost money. The network should be stabilized so that it can carry a losing show and still maintain an overall profit. Mr. Jensen has an important message he wants conveyed to the American people, and Howard Beale is conveying it. He wants Howard Beale back on the air tomorrow, and he wants him kept on. I would describe his position on this as inflexible. Where does that put us, Diana?"

She took papers out of her attaché case. "That puts us in the shithouse, that's where it puts us." She held up her sheaf of documents. "Do you want me to go through this?"

"Yes."

"Well," Diana said, "you'll all be getting your June reports within the week, but I have an advance sheet here. The Beale show Q score, which was forty-seven in the May book is down to thirty-three and falling. I won't go through the whole demographic breakdown, but most of this loss occurred in the child and teen and eighteen—thirty-four categories, which were once our core markets. 'The NBC Nightly News,' by contrast, has gone up to a twenty-nine Q, and, at this rate, will pass us by the end of July.

"Everybody here knows the Nielsen and share-trend scores, and Joe here will be breaking down the effects of this on his CPMs. Let me just capsulate our own AR reports which have been extensive. We may have already lost the teen-agers. They're a less addicted audience, and they've gone cold on Beale. It is the AR department's carefully considered judgment—and mine—that if we get rid of Beale, we should be able to maintain a very respectable share in the high twenties, possibly thirty with a comparable Q level.

The other segments on the Beale show—Sybil the Soothsayer, Jim Webbing, the Vox Populi—have all developed their own audiences. Our AR reports show without exception that it is Howard Beale that's the destructive force here. If we keep Beale on the air, it is our conservative estimate that we will drop to an eighteen share. Minimally, we are talking about a ten-point differential in shares. We all know the catastrophe—if Mr. Jensen will excuse the use of that word—that means in advertising revenues, but I think Joe ought to spell it out for us, anyway. Joe?"

"Ten points, are you kidding?" Donnelly said. "A twenty-eight share? That's eighty-thousand dollar minutes, and I think we could sell complete positions on the whole. As a matter of fact, we're just getting into the pre-Christmas gift-sellers and I'll tell you the agencies are coming back to me with four dollar CPMs. If that's any indication, you can figure the Beale show will be going for fifty thousand dollar minutes maybe. The difference between a twenty-eight and an eighteen? We're talking forty, forty-five million dollar loss in annual revenues."

"You guys want to hear all the flack I'm getting from affiliates?" Herb Thackeray said.

"We know all about it," Hackett said.

"And," Wheeler said, "you would describe Mr. Jensen's position on Beale as inflexible?"

"Intractable," Hackett said, "and adamantine."

"So what're we going to do about this Beale son of a bitch?" Nelson Chaney asked.

Hackett sighed. "I suppose we'll have to kill him."

There was a long contemplative silence.

"I don't suppose," Hackett said, "you have any ideas on that?"

"We don't want to implicate the network," Amundsen said. "This is, after all, a capital crime, and we're right now engaged in conspiracy."

"Well," Diana said, "what would you fellows say to an assassination?" She paused.

"I think," she said, "I can get the Mao Tse-tung people to kill Beale for us. As one of their programs. In fact, it'll make a hell of a kickoff show for the season. We're facing heavy opposition from the other networks on Wednesday nights, and 'The Mao Tse-tung Hour' could use a sensational show for an opener. The whole thing would be done right on camera in the studio. We ought to get a fantastic look-in audience with the assassination of Howard Beale as our opening show."

"Sounds good to me," Thackeray said.

"Let's check this out before we jump in," Walter Amundsen, the Legal Affairs man, said. "If Beale dies, what would be our continuing obligation to the Beale corporation? I know our contract with Beale contains a buy-out clause triggered by his death or incapacity."

"There must be a formula for the computation of a purchase price," Chaney said.

"Offhand," said Amundsen, "I think it was based on capitalization of earnings with the base period in 1975. I think it was fifty percent of salary plus twenty-five percent of the first year's profits multiplied by the unexpired portion of the contract. I don't think the show has any substantial syndication value, would you say, Diana?"

"Syndication profits are minimal," Diana Christensen said.

"You'll check out all the policies and our contracts with Beale anyway, Walter," Hackett said.

"Of course," Amundsen said, "but I remember the general terms pretty well."

"Well, the issue is," Hackett said, "shall we kill Howard Beale or not? I'd like to hear some more options on that."

"I don't see how we have any option," Diana said. "Let's kill the son of a bitch."

A few days later the lobby of the UBS building was bustling and crowded at 6:00 P.M. There were long lines of people, four abreast, guided by ushers who chatted with the waiting crowd. Gradually, the crowd was herded into elevators. At the fourth floor they were led out of the elevators, down the long carpeted corridors, past large wall photographs of TV stars, glass-enclosed control rooms and other showpieces of the network's electronic glory. Filing into the news show studio, they found seats in a rapidly filling auditorium. A camera crew was setting the cameras and checking the booms. The stage curtain was down.

After the warm-up the stage footlights came on and, as the clocked turned 6:30, an announcer strode out of the wings, bellowing happily at the audience.

"Ladies and gentlemen, let's hear it—how do you feel?"

*"We're mad as hell,"* the audience shouted, *"and we're not going to take this any more!"* Among them, happily shouting with all the rest, was the Great Ahmed Khan and some of his followers.

"Ladies and gentlemen," the announcer said, "The Network News Hour! With Sybil the Soothsayer, Jim Webbing and his It's-the-Emmes-Truth Department, Miss Mata Hari, tonight another segment of Vox Populi and starring—" (there was music and a flourish of drums) "—the mad prophet of the airways, *Howard Beale!*"

The music, played by a full symphony orchestra, soared to a crescendo.

The houselights went to black. The curtain rose slowly. The stained glass window on the bare stage was illuminated by a celestial shaft of light. Howard Beale, in his black suit and tie, strode from the wings, stood basking in the spotlight while the audience applauded.

A hush followed. And suddenly the hush was shattered by submachine gun fire. An embroidery of bleeding bullet holes perforated Howard Beale's shirt and jacket, and he pitched backwards, dead.


At 7:14 P.M., Wednesday, July 9, Diana Christensen was watching a bank of four color television monitors. On each was a network news program, NBC, CBS, ABC and UBS. The audio was on. There were headshots of Walter Cronkite, John Chancellor, Howard K. Smith, Harry Reasoner and Jack Snowden, who had replaced Howard Beale. Their faces were interspersed with the tapes of the horrible happening at UBS the day before. Out of the jumble of voices, Diana chose to listen to John Chancellor's account of the event. Television continued relentlessly on.

# PRODUCTION
# NOTES

# Cast

| | |
|---|---|
| Diana Christensen | FAYE DUNAWAY |
| Max Schumacher | WILLIAM HOLDEN |
| Howard Beale | PETER FINCH |
| Frank Hackett | ROBERT DUVALL |
| Nelson Chaney | WESLEY ADDY |
| Arthur Jensen | NED BEATTY |
| Great Ahmed Khan | ARTHUR BURGHARDT |
| TV Director | BILL BURROWS |
| George Bosch | JOHN CARPENTER |
| Harry Hunter | JORDAN CHARNEY |
| Mary Ann Gifford | KATHY CRONKITE |
| Joe Donnelly | ED CROWLEY |
| Walter C. Amundsen | JEROME DEMPSEY |
| Barbara Schlesinger | CONCHATA FERRELL |
| Milton K. Steinman | GENE GROSS |
| Jack Snowden | STANLEY GROVER |
| Caroline Schumacher | CINDY GROVER |
| Bill Herron | DARRYL HICKMAN |
| Arthur Zangwill | MITCHELL JASON |
| TV Stage Manager | PAUL JENKINS |
| Merrill Grant | KEN KERCHEVAL |
| Associate Producer | KENNETH KIMMINS |
| TV Production Assistant | LYNN KLUGMAN |
| Max's Secretary | CAROLYN KRIGBAUM |
| Audio Man | ZANE LASKY |
| Tommy Pellegrino | MICHAEL LIPTON |
| Willie Stein | MICHAEL LOMBARD |
| Herb Thackeray | PIRIE MacDONALD |
| TV Associate Director | RUSS PETRANTO |
| Lou | BERNARD POLLOCK |
| Sam Haywood | ROY POOLE |
| Edward George Ruddy | WILLIAM PRINCE |
| Helen Miggs | SASHA von SCHERLER |

# NETWORK

Robert McDonough ........LANE SMITH
Giannini .................THEODORE SOREL
Louise Schumacher ........BEATRICE STRAIGHT
Mosaic Figure ............FRED STUTHMAN
TV Technical Director ......CAMERON THOMAS
Laureen Hobbs ............MARLENE WARFIELD
Hunter's Secretary .........LYDIA WILEN
Narrator ..................LEE RICHARDSON

# Credits

Director . . . . . . . . . . . . . . . . . . SIDNEY LUMET
Producer . . . . . . . . . . . . . . . . . HOWARD GOTTFRIED
Original story and
   screenplay written by . . . . . PADDY CHAYEFSKY
Associate Producer . . . . . . . . FRED CARUSO
Original music composed
   and conducted by . . . . . . . ELLIOT LAWRENCE
Director of Photography . . . . . OWEN ROIZMAN, A.S.C.
Production Designer . . . . . . . . PHILIP ROSENBERG
Editor . . . . . . . . . . . . . . . . . . . ALAN HEIM
Costume Designer . . . . . . . . . THEONI V. ALDREDGE
Casting . . . . . . . . . . . . . . . . . . JULIET TAYLOR/MDA
1st Assistant Director . . . . . . JAY ALLAN HOPKINS
2nd Assistant Director . . . . . . RALPH SINGLETON
Camera Operator . . . . . . . . . . FRED SCHULER
Assistant Cameraman . . . . . . TOM PRIESTLEY, JR.
2nd Assistant Cameraman . . . GARY MULLER
Assistant Editor . . . . . . . . . . . MICHAEL JACOBI
Sound Editors . . . . . . . . . . . . JACK FITZSTEPHENS
                              SANFORD RACKOW
                              MARC M. LAUB
Re-Recordist . . . . . . . . . . . . . DICK VORISEK
Sound Mixer . . . . . . . . . . . . . JAMES SABAT
Set Decorator . . . . . . . . . . . . EDWARD STEWART
Still Photographer . . . . . . . . . MICHAEL GINSBURG
Key Grip . . . . . . . . . . . . . . . . KENNETH GOSS
Gaffer . . . . . . . . . . . . . . . . . . NORMAN LEIGH
Ms. Dunaway's Makeup . . . . . LEE HARMAN
Ms. Dunaway's Hair . . . . . . . SUSAN GERMAINE
Makeup Artist . . . . . . . . . . . . JOHN ALESE
Hair Stylist . . . . . . . . . . . . . . PHIL LETO
Costumers . . . . . . . . . . . . . . GEORGE NEWMAN
                              MARILYN PUTNAM

# NETWORK

Script Supervisor .......... KAY CHAPIN
Property Master ............ CONRAD BRINK
Location Coordinator ....... JOHN STARKE
Office Coordinator ......... CONNIE SCHOENBERG
Production Auditor ......... SELMA BROWN
Extra Casting .............. TODD-CHAMPION, LTD.


## FILMED IN PANAVISION®

Prints in Metrocolor


U.B.S. Video Logo by
Steve Rutt/E.U.E. Video Services


A
HOWARD                    PADDY
GOTTFRIED              CHAYEFSKY
        PRODUCTION

# The Making of
# NETWORK

The provocative and highly controversial theme of Metro-Goldwyn-Mayer's *Network*, by Paddy Chayefsky, is nothing less than the moral decline of modern American life. Producer Howard Gottfried says, "Our film deals with the destruction of the individual and traditional American ideals through a system dedicated to conformity, standardization, and the least common denominator."

Using as a vehicle television and its awesome power to manipulate popular thought, *Network*, directed by Sidney Lumet, tells its outrageously devastating story in both comedic and human terms, with a brilliant cast headed by Faye Dunaway, William Holden, Peter Finch, and Robert Duvall.

A less authoritative creative team might have fallen victim to the obvious pitfalls awaiting a motion picture that combined powerful social commentary with humor, but virtually everyone connected with *Network* has won the esteem of his peers and the respect of the moviegoing audience by refusing to compromise personal visions.

Paddy Chayefsky, who wrote *Network*'s original screenplay, cut his creative teeth in the heyday of live television in the 1950s. He wrote widely admired teleplays such as "The Bachelor

Party" and "The Catered Affair," which dealt with the pressures of married life—to name only two of his many award-winning scripts.

Chayefsky won his first Academy Award in 1955, for his screenplay for *Marty*, a film that totally revised motion picture corporate thinking by showing that the American-made "personal film" could be acceptable to American audiences. Other Chayefsky films include the movie adaptations of *The Bachelor Party, Middle of the Night,* and the cynically humorous *Americanization of Emily*. In 1971, the screenwriter again delighted film audiences with the devastating and bitterly funny movie *Hospital,* for which he won his second Academy Award.

Director Sidney Lumet's career has also been distinguished by a determination to meet controversy head on. His last film before *Network* was *Dog Day Afternoon,* a funny and ultimately tragic look at a desperate bank robbery gone wrong. He has also directed such powerfully realistic films as *Serpico, Long Day's Journey Into Night, The Pawnbroker, The Group,* and *The Hill.* Never a director to limit himself to one style of filmmaking, Lumet has also delighted audiences with lighter fare, such as *Murder on the Orient Express.*

The four stars of *Network* have had their share of challenging films as well. Faye Dunaway's career has included such outstanding films as *Bonnie and Clyde* and *Chinatown* (both earned her Academy Award nominations), as well as *The Arrangement, Three Days of the Condor, Puzzle of a Downfall Child,* and *Doc.*

William Holden began his career with an exceptional performance in Clifford Odets' *Golden Boy* and went on to films like *Stalag 17* (for which he won an Academy Award), *Sunset Boulevard*, *Born Yesterday*, and *Bridge on the River Kwai*.

Peter Finch has won England's Academy Award a record four times, and has surprised American audiences with his versatility and his refusal to shy away from controversial material. The Australian-born actor was nominated for an American Academy Award for *Sunday, Bloody Sunday* and has appeared in such other notable films as *The Nun's Story*, *The Abdication* (with Liv Ullmann), and *The Nelson Affair* (with Glenda Jackson).

Robert Duvall first came to the public's attention playing the *consigliore* to the Corleone family in *The Godfather*, a role he repeated in the excellent *The Godfather, Part II*.

In addition to the four stars, the cast includes such distinguished players as Beatrice Straight, William Price, Welsey Addy, Darryl Hickman, and Conchata Ferrell. Owen Roizman serves as director of photography (*The French Connection*, *Three Days of the Condor*, *Return of a Man Called Horse*) and Theoni V. Aldredge is the costume designer.

As Diana Christensen, the network's vice-president in charge of programming, Faye Dunaway finds one of the strongest roles of her career. Having ignored the movie-star preference for playing sympathetic characters, Miss Dunaway infuses her callous role with a bravado rarely seen on the screen today: Diana is sensual, cruel, passionate, ruthless, vulnerable, tough, and charming.

In the pivotal role of Howard Beale the network-news anchorman, Peter Finch creates a character of complexity and vision that challenges any preconceived notions of Finch's range as an actor. Chayefsky has written a modern-day prophet, a character filled with sound and fury, and the dramatic demands on the actor are extraordinary. It is to Finch's credit that he not only conveys the aura of dignified authority of his real-life counterparts on the major networks —Walter Cronkite, John Chancellor, Eric Sevareid—but is able to make even Howard Beale's mental collapse seem as convincing and as inevitable as his rebirth as the "Mad Prophet of the Airways."

As Max Schumacher, the president of the News Division whose career depends upon the whims of a giant communications corporation, William Holden presents us with a character of strength and integrity whose loyalty to his friend, Howard Beale, transcends his own interests. In a professionally dangerous but personally necessary gesture, Shumacher defies the network's corporation president.

Robert Duvall plays a hard-nosed senior corporation executive and hatchet man with a strength and menace that adds still another portrait to his gallery of character roles.

The filming of *Network* began in Toronto, in order to make use of the superb facilities of CFTO–TV Studios, one of the most complete and modern broadcasting plants on the continent.

Two enormous sound stages and a wide variety of control rooms, monitor booths, and other physical facilities necessary to the story were used. Using this real equipment made it possible for the filming to take place simultaneously on two separate floors of the building.

On the enormous sound stage on the street level Sidney Lumet filmed Peter Finch portraying network-news anchorman Howard Beale. The setting for "The Howard Beale Show" was elaborate and exaggerated in size and design. The dramatic figure of Beale was backed by a huge panel of stained glass, and he was outlined by a beam of white light that created what looked like a halo around his handsome, Romanesque head. Before him was a rapt audience of four hundred people. Two television cameras on cranes moved about the set like modernistic dinosaurs, circling, lifting, and dipping their camera heads. Covering this scene were the movie cameras, recording the anguish of Howard Beale, the reactions of the crowd, and the movements of the television cameras.

At the same time, in a small control room on the building's third floor, Sidney Lumet could also shoot a scene featuring William Holden, Faye Dunaway, and a group of actors playing TV executives and technicians. They were all intently watching the battery of twelve-inch TV monitor screens mounted on a control panel. The object of their attention was "The Howard Beale Show," *live*, as it was being broadcast two floors below them.

The CFTO–TV station in Toronto is new and extremely well equipped, and the management cooperated unstintingly in helping MGM people make *Network*, a motion picture about television, within the walls of a real television station.

The success of the filming in Toronto added to the realism and authenticity that mark all of Lumet's work.

It would have been impossible to have done this part of the filming in any New York network studio. So much material is broadcast daily from NBC, CBS, and ABC in Manhattan that none of the local sound stages could have been tied up for the necessary two weeks. Some preliminary inquiries were made before deciding to shoot these special scenes elsewhere, but MGM quickly realized that no area could be made available in New York for ten shooting days without seriously interrupting the flow of regular network programming.

After the completion of the sequences requiring the facilities of a real television station, the *Network* group did move to New York where the remainder of the film was made in specially designed offices and executive suites in the MGM Building. Through the wide-vista windows of this building the actual headquarters buildings of the three television networks—ABC, CBS, and NBC —can be seen in the immediate background. There was, at one period, some confusion among the passersby on 55th Street and the Avenue of the Americas when the MGM logo disappeared from the building and was replaced with the impressive logo of UBS, the United Broadcasting Systems invented by Paddy Chayefsky.

*Network,* completed seven full days ahead of schedule, is a joint production venture of Metro-

Goldwyn-Mayer and United Artists. It will be released as an MGM presentation by United Artists in the United States and Canada, and as a United Artists presentation abroad.

# The Story

The story of *Network* concerns the conversion of a highly esteemed but fading news anchorman into the biggest hit personality on television. It reveals the rarely seen machinery of network TV in a series of dramatic events—some outrageously funny, others terrifying in their social implications. The corruption of a network news broadcast, the sensationalizing of both entertainment and news programming, the pressures of personal ambition, the power struggles behind the cameras—all lead the story to its powerful climax.

The plot is triggered when Howard Beale's anguished behavior before the cameras turns him into an overnight hit and sets in motion behind-the-scenes corporate machinations.

Although Paddy Chayefsky's screenplay is about television, it implicitly says *j'accuse* to newspapers, magazines, motion pictures, and other forms of mass communication serving the average man or woman—who is often blindly led, fed, and bled by what the screen or printed page doles out in the guise of "news."

*Network* deals not only with the disintegration of a good man with a fine mind, but also with the plight of all men and women who must compromise and dissemble to survive in a highly competitive society, even if it means the sacrifice of individual and of human dignity.

# The Stars

## FAYE DUNAWAY is Diana Christensen

Faye Dunaway was born in Bascom, Florida, the daughter of John and Grace Dunaway. Her father was a career Army man, and consequently Faye's elementary and high-school education took place in such diverse locations as Utah, Florida, Germany, and other Army stopover spots. She attended the University of Florida, where she was active in the Drama Department, and, in her sophomore year, acted the tragic title role in *Medea*. In order to further pursue her interest in acting, she transferred to the Boston University School of Fine and Applied Arts, an academic institution that has graduated many of our top stars. She studied her craft there with Ted Kazanoff.

It was in Boston, while she was playing the leading role in *The Crucible,* that her director, Lloyd Richards, invited Elia Kazan and Robert Whitehead to see her performance and to audition her for their Lincoln Center Company. Under their aegis, she appeared in the Kazan production of Arthur Miller's *After the Fall* and in *But For Whom Charlie* and *Tartuffe*. Her performance in the American Place Theatre in *Hogan's Goat,* however, marked a turning point in her career. Producer Sam Spiegel saw her performance and signed her for her first film, *The Happening*, in which she played opposite Anthony Quinn. That was followed by a role as the earthy wife of a dirt farmer in Otto Preminger's *Hurry Sundown.*

She was then chosen by Arthur Penn to play Bonnie Parker opposite Warren Beatty in *Bonnie and Clyde*. Her next appearances were in John Frankenheimer's *The Extraordinary Seaman,* with David Niven, and in Norman Jewison's *The Thomas Crown Affair,* with Steve McQueen. Then came *A Place for Lovers,* with Marcello Mastroianni (directed by the late Vittorio de Sica), Elia Kazan's *The Arrangement,* Arthur Penn's *Little Big Man,* Jerry Schatzberg's *Puzzle of a Downfall Child,* Frank Perry's *Doc,* Stanley Kramer's *Oklahoma Crude,* and Richard Lester's *The Three Musketeers* and *The Four Musketeers.* She also recently starred in *The Towering Inferno, Three Days of the Condor, Voyage of the Damned,* and, of course, *Chinatown,* for which she was nominated for an Oscar.

Faye interrupted the routine of filmmaking in 1974 and returned to the stage to play Blanche in the Los Angeles Ahmanson Theatre revival of Tennessee Williams' *A Streetcar Named Desire.*

## WILLIAM HOLDEN is Max Schumacher

When William Holden adopted his screen name from a man who at the time was assistant managing editor of the *Los Angeles Times,* his choice unwittingly anticipated his current portrayal of another kind of journalist in *Network:* Max Schumacher, the president of the News Division of United Broadcasting Systems.

Born in O'Fallon, Illinois, the son of a prosperous chemist-manufacturer, he shed his given name, William Beedle, after a studio talent scout discovered him in a small part at the world-famous Pasadena Playhouse and arranged a screen test. Holden quickly secured the title role as a young boxer in Rouben Mamoulian's 1938 *Golden Boy*. When he was released as a first lieutenant after four years of service in the U.S. Air Corps during World War II, he fought his way to a leading position among Hollywood's finest acting and creative talents. His 1950 performance in *Sunset Boulevard* earned him an Academy Award nomination, and he received an Oscar for *Stalag 17* in 1953. He was among the ten top money-making film stars in 1954, 1955, and 1957.

Among his acclaimed and versatile performances, Holden has held leading roles in *Born Yesterday, The Country Girl, Love Is a Many Splendored Thing, Picnic, Bridge on the River Kwai, The World of Suzi Wong, The Counterfeit Traitor, The Devil's Brigade,* and *The Longest Day.* His most recent box-office smash was *The Towering Inferno.*

The role of a high-pressured executive in charge of news operations fits Holden well. Besides acting, he has major interests in the import-export trade, in electronics, in radios, in TV sets, and in racetrack investments. Part owner of the Mount Kenya Safari Club, a Hong Kong hotel, and other extensive real-estate holdings, Holden is familiar with the almost frantic activity that characterizes modern corporate organizations. He lives in East Africa for about five months each year, and also has a home in California.

# NETWORK

## PETER FINCH is Howard Beale

Filmgoers who recall Peter Finch as the perplexed doctor in John Schlesinger's powerful *Sunday, Bloody Sunday* will see the soft-spoken British gentleman actor tackle a completely different role—that of the beleaguered television news anchorman, Howard Beale—in *Network*. Curiously, he once held a job in a related field of journalism—he was a cub reporter for the *Sydney Sun* when he was trying to survive Australia's economic depression in his youth. To cope with hard times, he also took on such diverse jobs as vaudeville performer, radio actor, and itinerant "swagman."

Young Finch's affair with the *Sydney Sun* was a short-lived one; since that time he has frequently been on the other side of the journalistic exchange, the subject of countless press interviews about his many accomplishments. In 1960, the British Film Academy named him Best Actor for his performance in *Oscar Wilde*, and bestowed upon him the same award for his role in *No Love for Johnny*. In 1971, he won an Academy Award nomination for *Sunday, Bloody Sunday*.

Born in 1920, the son of the distinguished physicist Professor George Finch (a former mountaineer and member of the 1922 Leigh-Mallory Everest expedition), Peter was first exposed to acting while living with his grandmother in France.

After the depression, he served with the Australian Army in the Middle East. When his regiment shipped back to Australia, he organized a stage troupe for Allied servicemen dubbed "Finch's Follies." In 1946, Laurence Olivier and Vivien Leigh spotted his company of strolling players, called The Mercury (after Orson Welles), and secured an audition for him for *Daphne Laureola,* starring Dame Edith Evans, in London. His immediate success in the part brought him other roles in British theater, including *The Damascus Blade* with John Mills, *Captain Carvallo* with Diane Wynyard, and *Othello* with Orson Welles. Sir Michael Balcon, impressed by Finch's list of accomplishments, cast him for an important screen role in *Train of Events* in 1949, which in turn won him the part of the wicked Sheriff of Nottingham in Walt Disney's *Robin Hood.*

Finch signed with the Rank Organization in 1955 and played his first role for them, with Kay Kendall, in *Simon and Laura.* After more top spots in British films, he ensnared American cinema fans playing opposite Audrey Hepburn in Warner Brothers' *The Nun's Story.* He has since alternated between British and American pictures; he has made thirty-four in all. In addition to his prize-winning films, his recent credits include *Lost Horizon* and *The Abdication,* both with Liv Ullmann, *Something to Hide,* with Shelley Winters, and *The Nelson Affair,* with Glenda Jackson.

Peter, his vivacious wife Elthea, and their daughter Diana recently joined the British contingent living permanently in Hollywood.

## ROBERT DUVALL is Frank Hackett

Robert Duvall's unforgettable performance as the *consigliore* to Marlon Brando's Don Corleone in *The Godfather* won him an Academy Award nomination as Best Supporting Actor. He re-created the role in *The Godfather, Part II* with equal success. He has escaped being stereotyped, judging by such contrasting roles as the mentally retarded villager in *To Kill A Mockingbird,* the deadly accurate pistol wielder in *The Outfit,* a disturbingly silent dirt farmer in Faulkner's *Tomorrow,* and now as the coldly efficient executive of a national conglomerate in *Network.*

San Diego-born, Duvall decided to pursue acting with the encouragement of his father, a rear admiral in the U.S. Navy. After receiving a drama degree from Principia College in Illinois and serving two years in the Army, he studied with Sandy Meisner at the famed Neighborhood Playhouse in New York, supporting himself as a dishwasher, mail sorter, truck driver's helper, and clerk at Macy's.

His stage credits echo the diversity of his odd jobs. He appeared in Arthur Miller's *A View from the Bridge* and William Faulkner's *Tomorrow* at the Playwrights' Foundation Theatre, and acted in some seventy-five plays—in the theaters from off-off Broadway showcases to the Shubert Theatre, where he appeared in *Wait Until Dark.*

Duvall then returned to his native California, where he became a much sought-after character guest performer in such popular television shows as "Route 66," "Twilight Zone," "Naked City," "The Defenders," "The FBI," and "Mod Squad."

Robert Mulligan spotted him in a live feature for NBC, "Destiny's Tot," and cast him as the retarded neighbor in *To Kill A Mockingbird*, launching his film career.

Duvall manages to fulfill an astounding film schedule, plunging from one picture to the next, often without a pause. His distinguished screen credits include *Captain Newman, M.D.*, *The Godfather*, *The Godfather, Part II*, *The Chase*, *Countdown*, *The Detective*, *Bullitt*, *True Grit*, *The Rain People*, *M\*A\*S\*H\**, *TXH-1138*, *Tomorrow*, *The Conversation*, *Breakout*, *The Killer Elite*, and his most recent work, *The Seven Percent Solution*, soon to be released.

# The Writer

**PADDY CHAYEFSKY** is a two-time Academy Award winner, having received Oscars for *Marty* in 1955 and for *Hospital* in 1971.

Chayefsky has been one of America's leading literary figures for the past twenty-five years. He started his career as a writer of short stories, documentary films, and radio scripts. His fame was achieved, however, with his teleplays for Television Playhouse, including the well-remembered classics "Marty," "Holiday Song," "Bachelor Party," "Sixth Year," "The Catered Affair," and "Middle of the Night."

His screenplays, besides his two Oscar-winning efforts, include *Bachelor Party, The Goddess, Middle of the Night,* and *The Americanization of Emily.* Among his stage achievements are *Middle of the Night, The Tenth Man, Gideon, Passion of Josef D,* and *The Latent Heterosexual.*

# The Director

SIDNEY LUMET brings an extensive firsthand knowledge of television, as well as his formidable directorial skills, to *Network*. His most recent pictures were the critical and box-office hits *Serpico, Murder on the Orient Express,* and last year's *Dog Day Afternoon;* for which he received an Academy Award nomination.

Like screenwriter Paddy Chayefsky, Lumet is a veteran of television's "golden era." He became a staff director for CBS in 1950 and directed more than three hundred shows for the network in the succeeding five years. Among the memorable programs with which he was associated are "Mama," "Danger," "You Are There," "Omnibus," "Best of Broadway," "The Alcoa Hour" and "Goodyear Playhouse."

Lumet's film career began with his direction of the classic *Twelve Angry Men,* based on a television play. He then directed such diverse movies as *Stage Struck, That Kind of Woman, The Fugitive Kind, A View from the Bridge, Long Day's Journey Into Night, Fail-Safe, The Pawnbroker, The Hill, The Group, The Deadly Affair, Bye, Bye, Braverman, Last of the Mobile Hotshots, The Anderson Tapes, The Appointment, The Sea Gull, Child's Play,* and *The Offence*.

Lumet was an actor before he was a director; he made his show-business debut at the age of four with a role in a radio series directed by his father, the famed Yiddish actor Baruch Lumet.

While attending school in Manhattan, he continued to act regularly, primarily on the stage. He was in the Max Reinhardt production of *The Eternal Road* and made his screen debut as Sylvia Sidney's brother in *One Third of a Nation*. Broadway appearances include *Dead End, George Washington Slept Here,* and *My Heart's in the Highlands.*

After a four-year stint in the Army during World War II, Lumet returned to acting but also began directing, first with off-Broadway productions and summer stock. Among his stage directorial credits are *Caligula, Night of the Auk,* and the off-Broadway production of Shaw's *The Doctor's Dilemma.*

# The Producer

HOWARD GOTTFRIED produces his second film with *Network*; his first was Paddy Chayefsky's *Hospital*. Prior to that, Gottfried served as vice-president in charge of program development and production for Ed Sullivan Productions, active in both television and motion pictures.

From 1964 to 1967 Gottfried, as vice-president of United Artists Television (New York and California) in charge of production, supervised all United Artists TV programs, including such well-known ones as "The Fugitive," "The Outer Limits," "The Patty Duke Show," and "Gilligan's Island."

Gottfried broke into show business while serving as an attorney for many prominent theatrical figures. Gradually giving up his law practice, he began to produce in the New York theater, primarily off-Broadway; he now has over a dozen productions to his credit. Among the shows under his aegis were the American premiere of Sean O'Casey's *Purple Dust*, and *I Knock at the Door* and *Pictures in the Hallway*.

His production of John Dos Passos' *USA*, after running over a year in New York, toured successfully throughout the United States for several years.

# NETWORK

## Filmdom Creates a Fourth TV "Network"— United Broadcasting Systems

In real life, television networks are not created overnight. Unlike Athene, who sprang full-grown from the head of Zeus, giant networks are not instantaneously generated in the brain of some industrial wizard. America's three—NBC, CBS, and ABC—arrived at their present status through a long and convoluted period of growth, mergers, affiliations, and progressive development.

In the movies, however, anything is possible, and Paddy Chayefsky's fictional TV network, devised for Metro-Goldwyn-Mayer's *Network* and known as UBS (The United Broadcasting Systems), was brought to full flower in a matter of months.

With Paddy Chayefsky's very explicit script in hand, and acting under the leadership of director Sidney Lumet, the designer set about to create an impressive new network in the image of the three existing ones. For this purpose they took over several floors of the MGM Building, a sleek, modern skyscraper that happens to stand in the midst of what is known in New York as "Network Row." Through the windows of the executive suites one can clearly see the CBS office building directly across the street; two blocks to the south of them looms the ABC Building; and on the near horizon is the tall, slim RCA Building, which houses NBC and is part of Rockefeller Center.

An amusing incident occurred late one afternoon during the filming of *Network*. A scene was being shot in the office of William Holden, who portrays the president of the News Division at UBS. Through the huge windows one could see dusk falling and the street lights coming on. Forming a natural backdrop outside the windows was the towering RCA Building, its windows brightly lighted, giving a festive air to the darkening New York skies. On the movie set, a scene between Faye Dunaway and William Holden was just beginning. It was "Take 1," and there were several hours of filming ahead. Suddenly someone got the idea that at a given time the RCA lights would be turned off, and that this would ruin the continuity of the scene.

An assistant director got to the phone immediately and called the RCA Building's service offices. Naturally they were closed. He tried to reach the engineer's office, but the engineer wasn't at his desk. Finally he reached the security guards' quarters and, after being passed along from rank to rank like a military supplicant, he got to the head officer. Question: "What time do you turn off the lights in the offices?" The officer was immediately suspicious, and it took half an hour of explaining before he was convinced that the caller wasn't some burglar, or, worse yet, bomb terrorist, planning a heinous crime. The assistant film director never did get a specific reply from the guard, but when Sidney Lumet completed his scene around midnight, the RCA Building lights were still on.

Art director Phil Rosenberg converted the vacant floors of the MGM Building into offices and executive suites suitable for top network executives. He created a conference room, an executive dining room, reception areas, secretarial niches, and a projection room suitable for a fully operating television administration area.

At the lower end of the industry totem pole are the ushers. Not to be outdone by the other networks, designer Theoni V. Aldredge created the ushers' uniforms as well as the clothes worn by the stars. These were smartly tailored cadet-blue uniforms with lapel patches bearing the UBS logo. The logo itself bore the UBS legend in stripes of red and blue against a white background.

Naturally, these patches had to be made to order for the film. Unlike mass-produced patches, which sell for about a dollar, these had to be hand-crafted at more than five dollars each. Needless to say, in the final days of the filming, these patches began to disappear. Such was the prestige connected with *Network* that everyone wanted one for a souvenir!

## "I Can't Remember Working This Hard and Feeling So Good"

"It was quite simply the best script I had read in years," says Academy Award-winning actor William Holden of his current film, Metro-Goldwyn-Mayer's *Network,* by Paddy Chayefsky. "It's filled with passion and outrage," he continues. "I admire those qualities in writing, and we rarely see them on the screen anymore."

In *Network,* Holden, who co-stars with Faye Dunaway, Peter Finch, and Robert Duvall, plays an honest television executive forced to compromise his own integrity. "The film gives me the opportunity to say something about the way we live right now. Peter Finch plays a good, close friend whose sanity is threatened by events, and Faye Dunaway plays a very modern personality without a soul. We're all characters who are living out the consequences of the headlines," says Holden, "and I think audiences are going to be knocked out by the film."

Holden, who now makes his home in Kenya, considers the half year he spends out of the Hollywood environment an important contribution to keeping his own sanity. "I work with animals, on a reserve, keeping more than three hundred species of wildlife roaming free over the terrain. The whole venture is done with the cooperation of the Kenyan government, and it's an integral part of the ecological integrity of the country."

In addition to assuring the continuation of rare species, Holden's ranch assistants monitor the food and water supplies available, sometimes moving entire herds hundreds of miles to areas that can better support them and where their chances of survival are greater.

"The greatest enemy of the wild kingdom is man," Holden says. "Hunting is only a part of the problem. In the past few years, governments have taken notice of their wildlife populations and have tried to save endangered species by limiting the hunting season or reducing the hunter's bounty allowance. But great damage is also done by the growth of cities, and by industrial development. If the bird or animal is forced to invade new territories in search of food and water, it may very well throw the newly found habitat into an imbalance that threatens the existence of the native species. It's a very complicated situation."

During his five or six months away from Hollywood, Holden fills his days with working on his ranch and enjoys the quiet serenity of the evenings. This is when Holden does his reading, and among the books and magazines there are always a few scripts that have been sent to him from California.

Perhaps it is the basic security that Holden enjoys, and the serenity with which he can read and evaluate a script, that have led to the wisdom of his selections. Certainly he is not infallible, but the number of flop films he has chosen is miniscule compared to the record of most actors. His latest, *Network,* may well top all the others, not only as a screenplay, but also as an actor's vehicle.

"*Network* was an experience," Holden said a few weeks after the grueling shooting schedule was completed. "We were exhilarated and exhausted at the same time. I can't remember working this hard—emotionally—for a film *and* feeling this good about it. There's something about both Sidney [Lumet, the director] and Paddy [Chayefsky, the writer] that inspires good work. They both refuse to compromise, and that comes across in the films they make.

"There's a great deal of discussion in the film about morality—the choices we make as human beings and the consequences of those choices. I think it's important to come to terms with those questions. It's not a matter of finding an easy answer, but we do have to admit that complex problems exist."

Holden credits his co-actors with helping to create an atmosphere of trust that allowed extraordinary performances to emerge. "It was strange," says Holden, breaking into a cautious smile. "Peter [Finch] had to go crazy right before our eyes, and Faye [Dunaway] is playing the sort of unsympathetic part actors are never supposed to accept. It took quite a bit of courage for these actors to play the roles they did. Mine was really the easiest—a good man caught in circumstances he thinks he can't control.

"This is the second film I've done with Faye—she's a marvelous actress. I know you hear that she's difficult, but the only difficult thing about Faye is that she demands total commitment of herself and others. I find that invigorating, and I'm grateful we shared so many scenes. She makes you take yourself to your limit."

Does Holden have any doubts that the American public is ready for a film as uncompromising as *Network*? "Not at all," says Holden. "I think moviegoers want to be confronted with human truths—they want to think and feel. That's what makes *Network* important, and I think it will come across."

# NETWORK

## Faye Dunaway:
## An Actress of the Seventies

Jack Nicholson, after working with Faye Dunaway in *Chinatown,* described the actress by saying, "She's a gossamer grenade. She's not saving anything for later. She's open to the big jolt— she wants it. She gets hurt that way, but it's a useful kind of hurt. She's a brave woman, a very free woman."

Dunaway is, without question, the actress for the 1970s. Intelligent, sensual, witty, she radiates some of the flamboyance sadly missing from the screen since the reign of the celluloid *grande dames* of the Thirties. In MGM's *Network,* she plays the ultimate modern woman: a bitch goddess devoid of morals, with a complicated neurotic streak as wide as the Grand Canyon.

While Paddy Chayefsky, who wrote *Network,* admits to having had several actors refuse to appear in unsympathetic roles, Faye jumped at the chance. "I'm an actress. I do not play myself on the screen; I'm there to convey another emotion. Diana Christenson is a woman who seemingly has everything but truly has nothing. She is a woman without a center."

While agents and friends worried that her characterization of Diana would cause audiences to reject her, Faye remained unruffled. "I do what pleases me. I was happy to be in *The Towering Inferno* and *Three Days of the Condor* because they represent a kind of straight-out entertainment movie that is at the very heart of the industry. But I don't want to restrict myself to those kinds of films. *Network* is a strong movie with a difficult message, but it's because of its strength and courage that I wanted to do it."

Because of her soaring talent, Faye has often been termed difficult by her directors. In a now-famous *Rolling Stone* article, Roman Polanski took off against Dunaway in a diatribe that included criticism of her performance in *Chinatown*. Although she was honored for that role by an Academy Award nomination, the actress says she was deeply hurt by Polanski's remarks.

"Nothing rolls off my back. I get hurt too easily," she concedes. Even the high praise offered to her by other directors, such as Arthur Penn (*Bonnie and Clyde*) and Sidney Pollack (*Three Days of the Condor*), cannot fully undo the damage.

"I want people to be kind to people," she says simply. "I cannot understand why we all aren't nice to one another. I find life so often assaultive, and it is so much safer to react to the assault with rage than hurt. Who wants to be that vulnerable?" She adds, smiling, "I'm afraid my view of the world is very childlike. We should all be nice and play. Why can't we? I had such enormous love as a child. Such kindness. I think what has shocked me so all my life is not finding that in the world."

Faye was born thirty-four years ago in the back woods of Florida, and she grew up on Army posts in Germany and the United States. She compensated for her parents' early divorce by plunging into the dream of acting. "I can't remember when I didn't want to be an actress," she says. After a short period at Boston University, Faye moved to New York to be part of the Lincoln Center Repertory Theatre headed by Elia Kazan. Upon completing her three years' training, Faye went on to a startling performance in *Hogan's Goat* for the American Place Theatre, and to Broadway in *A Man For All Seasons*. It was during this period that Otto Preminger spotted her for stardom.

"In those days," she says, "I believed in the American dream of success—that it brought happiness. I believed that to be a movie star you should be thin and blonde and that after that everything would fall into place."

When everything did *not* fall into place, Faye abandoned America for Europe and a series of highly publicized love affairs. "I used men as buffers against the world," she explains. " 'Keeping Faye Safe,' it's called. And I kept Faye safe at all costs. I never walked away bleeding from a relationship, because I allowed them to continue long after they were over so I could prepare myself for the moving on. My bleeding took place while they were ending. I have always, in retrospect, been able to pinpoint the exact moment when a love affair was essentially over for me. But I couldn't let go. I was so afraid of being alone."

### Peter Finch Plays the Role of His Career in Network

"You know, I really retired from films for a few years before agreeing to this project," says

# NETWORK

Peter Finch, taking a short break from the grueling shooting schedule needed to complete Metro-Goldwyn-Mayer's *Network*. "I simply turned my back on acting and went down to my farm in Jamaica and played gentleman farmer. But I couldn't stand the idleness, and when I first read this incredible script, I knew I had to be a part of the project."

Casting a quick glance at *Network's* synopsis makes it clear why Finch could not overlook the chance to play a television anchorman who goes crazy on the evening news. In essence, *Network* deals with the corruption of honest news, the sensationalizing of entertainment programming, the pressures of personal ambition, and the power struggles behind the TV cameras. The role of Howard Beale offers Finch the opportunity to play a complex and magnificent character, a kind of full-blown hellion rarely seen on the American screen.

Tanned, relaxed, and sitting apart from the elaborate television set that served as the background for *Network*, Finch conveys little of the tormented character he plays on the screen. It was not until the director, Sidney Lumet, called Finch back to the lights that the Australian-born actor took on the trappings of a man caught in the terrors of schizophrenia.

"Some people may think Beale is insane," Finch allows, choosing his words as carefully as a Gabor sister might choose a diamond. "But I don't think so. I think what happened to Howard Beale was a 'streak of sanity.' Certainly he seems to go crazy right there on national television, but in another sense, that break from sanity allows

Beale to become something of a modern-day prophet.

"What I admire in writers," adds Finch, "is the passion to take a moral stand. All the great writers had that—Voltaire, Chekhov, Dostoevski. Today I think it's remarkable that Solzhenitsyn should be alive and writing the way he is. Unfortunately, he isn't appreciated the way he should be.

"It's remarkable, too, in this day and age when everything is so gray and there's so much prevarication about good and evil, that he should write so strongly about right and wrong. I like that.

"Paddy has some of that," Finch continues, mulling over the script of Network in his head before completing the statement. "Paddy has something I call divine madness. There's a manic quality in his work that I adore. I see that in Network with Beale."

Although Finch has played such outstanding roles as Iago in Othello and Tregorian in The Sea Gull, the actor insists that Network offers one of the strongest roles of his distinguished career. "In the theater we can expect to make statements, but rarely is that possible in film. I've done some good movies, but films are so monosyllabic—there's no language with which you can manipulate thought. If you want to go to an extreme example, there's Taxi Driver, which is totally monosyllabic, although I must say Americans have raised this kind of dialogue to eloquence.

"In Network, though, I have long speeches that truly get to the heart of emotions—and politics. It's very powerful. And rare. In Bloody Sunday, I remember having one good speech at the end, and I think Glenda [Jackson] had a rather fine one with her mother, but that was all. Paddy's writing is filled with indulgent language. He's a very moral writer."

Finch dismisses the notion that the general populace is not concerned with questions of morality. He cites both the continuing acceptance of the "great masters" and the flood of Watergate books as evidence that they are. "Obviously people still care about right and wrong, because all the great writers still sell. We live in a snide age, and one would think they wouldn't, but then there are all those Nixon books, too. There's a very moral lesson in those books—they're really about the wages of sin, aren't they? I'm convinced we still have a medieval respect for the problems of right and wrong.

"I do think it's possible for a society to put aside morality for a time," Finch adds. "The Germans certainly put it aside during Hitler's reign. I have a friend in Jamaica, a very fine lawyer, who once said to me, 'You must remember, people get tired of morality.' Countries often change their political stance because they're tired of individual liberty. I have never thought about it before. It takes work and struggle to have personal freedom, and people get tired. It's much easier to find someone else to tell us what to do. But when that happens, there's a resurgence that comes along, and we say, 'Hey, who is that guy with a pistol and why is he pushing me around?' "

Finch, who recently sold his Jamaican farm land, cherishes the turmoil manifested by a country struggling to find a new order. "I lived in Switzerland for quite a long time," he explains, "and although it was quite beautiful, it was dreadfully boring. All the problems were swept off the very clean streets and it was very clinical. I never felt a part of Switzerland the way I did Italy or England.

"We went from Switzerland to Jamaica, which was full of problems, but somehow I found the challenge stimulating and refreshing. There's humanity in Jamaica. I'm not saying Switzerland is inhuman, but it lacks energy. They've had three hundred years of going in one direction, and they are overly secure."

Finch, with his Jamaican-born wife Elthea and their five-year-old daughter Diana, are now planning a permanent move to Los Angeles. "We're remodeling a house." Finch laughs. "I've left the entire project up to Elthea. The last time I was there to deal with it, I took one look at the construction workers, who acted like they had been trained by Mack Sennett, and fled the premises!"

Upon completing *Network*, Finch plans to concentrate his efforts on a book he's been writing for some time. "I think I have the title—*Chutzpah*. It's really a collection of experiences I've had, people I've met, all tacked together. I'm not a professional writer, and writing comes very slowly to me, so I'm doing this in the same way I read that Chekhov wrote his stories—a bit here and a bit there."